D1282461

How to Succeed
in Company Politics

The Strategy of Executive Success

EDWARD J. HEGARTY

Management and Training Consultant
Formerly Director of Sales Training,
Appliance Division,
Westinghouse Electric Corporation

McGRAW-HILL BOOK COMPANY

New York • Toronto • London • San Francisco

WILLIAM MADISON RANDALL LIBRARY UNC AT WILMINGTON

HOW TO SUCCEED IN COMPANY POLITICS

Copyright © 1964 by McGraw-Hill Inc. All Rights Reserved.
Printed in the United States of America. This book, or parts
thereof, may not be reproduced in any form without permission of
the publishers. *Library of Congress Catalog Card Number* 64-16845

11-VBVB-75

07-027844-X

HF5500
.H393

Preface

THE MOST HUSH-HUSH SUBJECT IN BUSINESS

In its August, 1963, issue *Business Management* used this headline and the paragraph that follows to explain what that subject was.

Call up the President of any company in the United States. Ask to speak with him about his company's profits, its personnel policies, or its plans for growth. Chances are he'll be glad to talk to you. Ask him to discuss company politics, however, and chances are you'll get dead silence, followed by some vague, embarrassed indication that he knows absolutely nothing about the subject.

This is the reaction the editors ran into in trying to develop an article aimed at helping company presidents cope with company politics, to curb it or to slant it so the company benefits.

In doing the research for this book I experienced this same reaction. Men talked about company politics, but always with

iii

136080

the admonition, "Don't quote me." And so in these pages I use the quotes without the names. The best definition I heard of company politics was this, "Company politics is the byplay that occurs when one man or a group of men want to advance themselves or their ideas regardless of whether or not those ideas would help the company."

This definition indicates that some politics may help the company, that other kinds may hurt. Executives agree on this idea. It is not all bad, and it is not all good. But it is all active. Both the company politician and the party politician consider events and ask, "How can I make capital out of this?" There is this difference—the party politician is concerned with people, all of the people. He has a simple belief that, if enough people go to the polls, he will be elected. The company politician is concerned with the RIGHT people. He feels that, if he can get the votes of the RIGHT people by showing them an image of competence, he will get that better job. This type of political action may make him appear to be shrewd, scheming, cunning, but most of the time he has to know the score. If he doesn't, Number One's interests might go into a slump.

Of course, in itself the ability to use political techniques does not make a successful executive. But an executive who does not have political know-how is as handicapped as one who does not show up at the office at all. He is on the way to being a dead duck.

HOW THIS BOOK WAS WRITTEN

I have seen much of company politics. I've worked for large and small companies and as a consultant to both large and small. I have hired hundreds of young men, trained them and helped to place them. I have worked with men who have gone up to the top, others who have been eased out, others who didn't quite make it, and some few of that amazing species who get by without putting out any effort at all.

Some of these men were brilliant, others stupid. Both kinds went up and both kinds went out. But, while they were on the merry-go-round, all were politicking their best for little old Number One.

Now why were these men playing politics? Wasn't it because they understood that a man does not get to the top in business on ability alone, or hard work alone, or on a full complement of the storybook virtues alone? These men knew that they had to have something else working for them.

What is this something else?

When I interviewed executives in higher salary brackets about this something else, I started my inquiry with, "What advice would you give a young man about handling himself in company politics?" I reasoned that, because of the jobs they held, these men had successfully handled themselves in the politics of their companies, and their advice should be helpful. It was and, what is more, they did not hesitate to talk. Some said, "We don't have any of it in our company, and so I can't help you much but, when your book is published, I want a copy." In one case, when I prefaced my question with, "You probably don't have politics in your company," the executive broke in to ask, "Who says we don't? If we didn't have it, what kind of company would it be; nobody ambitious, nobody wanting to get ahead?"

When I told businessmen I met on planes and at meetings, "I am writing a book on company politics," I did not have to ask, "Do you have any ideas on the subject?" Out the ideas came and these are duly recorded in this book. The wording of one bit of advice to young men that was repeated over and over was

Keep your nose clean, and...

The "keep your nose clean" had nothing to do with ablutions or handkerchiefs. It could have been better stated perhaps as "keep out of trouble, and...." The advice following the "and" varied. Some bits were facetious like the one that went, "Keep your nose clean and vote Republican." Some executives will ask, "What's facetious about that?" They know that many a potential top executive has gone down the drain because he didn't think right about party politics. But party politics is but one of the bits of advice that followed the "and." The others will be explained in detail. For I asked these men to give me specific suggestions. Let's say a man advised, "Tell him to steer clear of politics." I then asked, "How would you advise him to do that?" It is through such verbal give and take that I got the material presented on the following pages. This book will do two things:

One, bring you the advice of these men who have gone through the mill, and

Two, explain how to follow the advice given.

I hope that the suggestions will be helpful to you.

Edward J. Hegarty

Contents

part 1

How to Check on What to Do

Before you start off politicking, making speeches, shaking hands, and kissing babies, let's take a look at company politics and examine how it can affect you in relation to:

What you can hope to make out of it,

How you shape up in the contest,

What's ahead of you where you are, and

Whether or not you should become a company politician or one of the help that can live a happy, useful life without the pressure, tension, or ulcers that striving might bring to you.

1

Leave Us Not Kid Ourselves

You get in by having what the job requires.

You advance to some extent by doing a good job on the work you are supposed to do.

But, to a larger extent, you advance in an organization through *politics*.

Now, politics is *not* a naughty word—it's a fact of business life, as it is of our national life.

Last year I heard the president of the U.S. Chamber of Commerce make a plea to businessmen to get involved in party politics: "If our kind of citizens don't take an interest," he said, "the others will. And what is the result? The others will be running things their way, not our way."

Many of the listeners agreed with what the man said, but there was no rush to sign up. They were going to continue to sit on their fat back porches and let the world be run by that other kind of people who would get off dead center and do something.

Get involved in company politics

If that speaker from the U.S. Chamber of Commerce had suggested that the listeners get involved in the politics of their respective companies, he would have come closer to home. For most of them were then involved whether or not they wanted to be. They accept the fact that politics will determine to some degree how far they advance in their companies. This may not be the storybook picture of how the executive gets to the top. But that is how it is.

What they tell you ain't so

Most success books tell you that, if you want to advance in business, you must work hard, develop your mental power, stoke up your enthusiasm, keep your eye on the ball. Advertisements advise you to avoid BO, halitosis, and greasy, messy hair and you have it made. This advice is not entirely haywire. It's good as far as it goes. Any advancement in a company calls for hard work and these other things, but it calls for more than that. And that plus is politics—getting the votes of the right people when those votes are needed.

Is it good politics?

You may think it is an unusual combination when we put the words "good" and "politics" together. For most of us don't think of politics as a good thing. But it is a good word. We have politics in every form of life. How about the family? Don't all conspire to get dad to buy the car that's big enough for the family instead of the little red bug that he has his heart set on? You have the same thing in the clubs you belong to, the PTA, the church groups; and you have it at the office. Only at the office you are playing more for keeps.

Small and big business

You may say this political stuff applies only to big business, the large corporations. But consider this case, one of my friends with a partner opened a bar and grill. They both worked in the place. After a month or so I asked my friend, "How do you like your partner?"

He said, "Ed, he won't sweep out the back room, always leaves it for me to do. Wants people to think that he owns the place."

"What do you want people to think?" I asked.

He laughed, "That I own it."

Each tried to give the impression to the customers that he was the owner. When they hired one waitress, she played one of them against the other. When they hired the second waitress, they had the two girls against the bosses. You say politics is only in large outfits? Well, forget that. It's in every business.

Low and top jobs

A young friend of mine just out of college took a job in the accounting department of a company. After six months he told me, "I can't take this industry job. I'm going back to school and study to be a veterinarian."

I asked why a job that looked promising a few months before had turned sour. "When I take a company's money for doing a job, I want to do a full day's work. My associates on this job complain that I'm turning out too much work and they are pressuring me all day to slow down. I can't take that."

Is that politics? Yes, and it's a bad kind, you agree.

You may say, "I'm too far down the line to be bothered by company politics. I don't want to set the world on fire. I just want to keep this 8-to-5 job I have." This sounds reasonable, but no matter what type of job you want, there is politics involved in getting and keeping it. Let's say that you are not overly ambitious, you have a soft snap and you'd like to keep it from now to social security. But let's further assume that the boss thinks this is a good spot for the brother-in-law. What chance do you have of holding on? You are on the same spot as the truly ambitious, into politics whether you like it or not.

There is no politics in my company

I talked to a number of personnel experts about politics in company management. Some of these said, "There is none of it in our company."

I asked one who made this statement, "Name a man who was recently promoted in the middle management of your company."

He named a man.

I asked, "What was his background?"

"He was the assistant to the man who was made vice-president."

"How long had he worked for this boss?"

"Oh, he had been this man's assistant for years, as the boss moved up through the various jobs."

"Throughout the company, would the others think of this man as the vice-president's man?"

"You call that politics?" he laughed. "I call it good management."

OK, perhaps it is, but it is good politics too.

On one job I had it was my duty to give an executive just hired his indoctrination. I took him through the factory, gave him a presentation on the organization chart, and did the usual things that were called for. During the presentation the man asked me, "Is there any politics in this company?"

I admitted there was. "But it may not be the kind of politics you have been led to believe exists in a company like this. In this place nobody is always trying to stick a knife in your back."

I don't think the man believed me. He thought that was a part of my pitch. But one day he told me, "Ed, this is my fifth anniversary here."

I congratulated him for he had done well in the five years, moved from one job to another, always up.

"One thing you told me on that first day," he went on, "that I have always remembered."

"What's that?"

"You said that nobody here would try to stick a knife in my back. You know I didn't believe you when you said it, but in the five years I have found it true."

"How about the politics?" I asked.

"Oh, that's here. We are inclined to clique together by departments, some of us eat lunch together every day, others play bridge with their wives, some play golf, others bowl. But you get to know people that way, and when a promotion is up, you'd rather trust a fellow you know with it than someone you don't know, wouldn't you?"

"Is this politics the insidious thing that you thought it was when you came to work for us?"

"No. It helps the company, I'm sure. A fellow that's into politics shows he can make friends. I'm sure management uses it. If a man is competing with another, he is inclined to do a better job, isn't he?"

He is, of course.

The promotable have it

Let's assume you work for a company and I ask why a man was promoted. I might get this answer, "He knows his way around." OK, what does that mean?

Another is, "People like him."

Why do they like him?

Another is,

"He's got what it takes."

Well, what has he got that it takes? Put those three answers together and they say he is a good politician, for doesn't the good politician know his way around? Isn't he well liked? Hasn't he got what it takes?

Then some answers will come closer to the truth. They will tell you,

"He's a good politician."

You ask, "So it takes a ward heeler to get ahead in this outfit? The kind of guy that goes about shaking hands and kissing babies?"

The question may indicate you are not too hep.

It pays to know the score

To move up in a company a good politician understands what makes it go. One personnel man put it, "If he has to offend somebody, he wants to offend the right people."

The other day I asked the president of a small company some questions. He asked, "Ed, have you ever read our annual report?" I admitted I hadn't. I didn't know the company had one. I could admit that as an outsider, but let's assume I was an employee and had been working for the company six months, and the boss asked me that question. What would he have thought if I had answered that way? That I didn't have much interest, perhaps. And that would be a mark against me. For, if you are to go up in a company, you have to have that interest.

Not long ago I looked at an organization chart of a company. I saw that one of my friends reported to another man. "Then this man is Charlie Owens' boss?" I asked.

My informant laughed, "Nobody bosses Charlie Owens," he said.

So, OK, the chart didn't show what it was supposed to show. Charlie Owens was a doer who ran things. And, according to the informant, he ran more than the chart showed he did.

But what brought out this fact? A question? And it is through such questions that you find out what makes your company tick. Look at it this way. You are spending your valuable time with this company. They are paying you, of course, but you want training, you want advancement. And, if the setup is such that you can't get either, you may have to move.

The moral of all this is that the fellow who wants to get to the top has to learn to read between the lines, to hear the things that are not said, to constantly check on the changes as the power shifts.

The grandstand moves

Let's say that you once worked for a company. You meet one of the men who worked in your office at the company. He says, "Pete, you ought to be glad you are not working there now." He is telling you that things have changed, isn't he? And that perhaps he was not on the right side in the changes. "How did Joe Whosis make out in the shuffle?" you ask.

"Got a promotion out of it, the lucky so-and-so."

This is company politics. Perhaps small time but, as you go up in the company, the small-time politics gets bigger-time, and the play is more for keeps. To be with the outs might mean that you are out of the company completely.

Shame of industry?

Sylvia Porter who syndicates a column, "Your Money's Worth," devoted one column to the subject, "Executive Turnover, Shame of Industry." She made the point that 41 per cent of the middle-management executives under fifty, making a salary of at least $20,000 per year, had quit their last job after holding it only 24 to 36 months. And 78 per cent of the group resigned their last post before they had been on it ten years. Many of these executives were offered better jobs, others were asked to resign, some were fired, others eased into jobs that held no promise and so they quit. But all understood the signals that told them to get out and get going. Most of the men were good men, knew the business, worked hard, were loyal, had much to contribute. But they went out. Why? Because they backed the wrong horse, paid no attention to the horses at all, or a better horse came along and they mounted that. Is this a shame of industry? Maybe "yes" and maybe "no." In some cases the companies lost good men. In others deadwood was cut out. But in most cases the executives that went over the hill got in wrong with the ins.

The ins and the outs

Any company is made up of these groups, the ins and the outs. Call them cliques, factions, or use more uncomplimentary names. In most cases one clique is in favor of this, another in favor of something else, and the battle is on. But this competition is not all bad for the company. The group that is for expansion knows it is working for the best interests of the company. The group for the *status quo* is certain its plan is best. Nobody is committing any sins against the company— it's all holy-pure-commendable. And while the two groups go about politicking in their cause, you take sides or you sit on the fence. But, whatever you do, it pays to do it so adroitly that you don't make enemies. You listen, you ask questions, you make no strong statements. Thus even on the sidelines you play your part in company politics.

Why this politics gets its bad name

One reason company politics gets its bad name is because it is an alibi, an out. The wife of the man who doesn't get the promotion asks, "Why didn't you get it?" He replies, "Lousy politics." It may be that the man who got the job was better-equipped, but the answer saves face for the loser. The man who is fired from a job gives a similar answer when anyone asks why. Let's say you have a man in the office who is holding a job without knowing anything about it. Ask any lowly clerk, "Why do they have that jerk on the job?" In most cases the clerk will answer, "I dunno, he must know where they bury the dead."

That's another way of giving politics an assist. And so pull and partiality and preference can take the rap for almost anything that happens, even though it does not always check with truth.

One man told me, "Politics is reprehensible to me, but I've got to know what is going on and even get involved at times." Another said, "An executive without political know-how is like the little black sheep in the song, the ones that lost their way." To some politics is fun, to others distasteful, but it is alive to everybody who wants to hold on or go up in business.

You need politics, plus

Leave us not kid ourselves either about what is needed to get to the top. The things that the self-improvement books advise—attitude, conformity, willingness, ability—all are good. But, even if you are loaded with them, you can't possibly make it without politics. You go up faster if you are on the right side, in with the right crowd, have the right friends, and are one of our boys. An outsider might say, "It's a shame. A fellow oughta get ahead on his ability and talent."

I admit this is a sound idea. But, if you want that kind of setup, start a business of your own. And even so you better do all of the work yourself.

When you came to work for your company, nobody told you this. But you weren't around long before you sensed it. And you'll have politics as long as you work for and with others. You're stuck with it. You don't have to parade about carrying banners that proclaim, "We want Ajax." But you get on Ajax's side if that is the side your boss is on. And, whether or not you like it, you are on a bandwagon. In time with experience you will know which wagon to get on and which horn to blow.

But don't let this discourage you. It's been this way for a long time. Everybody competing with you is in the same fix.

So——

1. Face it. There is politics in every company. It affects every job.

2. You'll find it in both the low and high echelons. As you go up, it gets tougher.

3. It's not all bad for the company. Some types of politics are good for the business.

4. If you want to hold onto the soft job you now have, you have to play politics.

5. If you want to advance to a better job, you have to play politics.

You know this, I'm sure, but let's examine what advancement you can expect.

2

How Far Do You Want to Go?

What are you willing to settle for?

That's a good question. Jokingly, one of my friends says, "I wish I had started out in life to be a hobo. I believe I would have been good at that."

Here is a story to prove even that is not easy. One hobo was complaining to another about the hobo's life, moving from place to place, hopping rides on freight trains, sleeping in cold and dirt, bumming handouts for food. The other listened to his complaints and asked, "Why don't you settle down, get yourself a job and get away from all this?"

"What," asked the other, "and admit I'm a failure?"

The man was complaining he had it tough. But he had settled for being a hobo and he meant to stick to it.

Ask yourself that question, "What am I willing to settle for?" Up the ladder in your company there are jobs for which you can equip yourself, some big, some not so big. At what level would you be satisfied?

Perhaps you are discouraged by this idea that it takes more than following the advice in the self-improvement books to get ahead in business.

Inspirational books tell you to set your sights high, to aim for any job you want. You can do that, of course, but is that realistic, does it make sense? Let's ask this question. It is lifted from a speech to management trainees:

"Are you sure you want to be an executive?"

The speech then goes on to ask, "Are you sure you are willing to undergo the self-discipline, the sacrifice, the day in and day out hard work, the midnight oil, the weekend hours, the constant self-analysis, the challenge that being an executive calls for?"

That doesn't sound like wine and roses, does it? But the road to the top calls for that and more.

And like the speaker I ask in my words, "Are you sure you want to get up into those higher brackets?"

Your answer to that question might be, "Yes, if I can do it honestly, with integrity, governed by high moral principles."

That's a high-sounding answer and cynics might ask you, "Are you kidding?"

But men do move up who have honesty, integrity, and moral principles. And what others can do you can too. But then ask yourself another question, "Do I need to get to the top to be happy?"

Some men do and some don't. I know one man whose associates say, "That guy will never be satisfied until he is running this outfit." There are many men like that. They know there is only one top job and they are shooting for it continuously. Others are content to be close to the top. One man told me, "I don't want the top man's job. Too many headaches. As long as I got a private office, a secretary, and work I like and can do acceptably, some pressure but not too much, I'm happy."

What's wrong with that? Nothing at all for that man.

But, you, would you be content with that?

One trouble with aiming at that type of job is that some day you may be taking orders from men who started even with you or perhaps years behind you. Not long ago an executive confessed, "The toughest job I ever had was to tell the wife that I was now reporting to that guy. I hired him, I trained him, and now he's my boss."

Then too when you get that job you want you may be caught in a bind and forced to take sides in a fight for a job up above, a fight that jeopardizes your sweet setup. But that is politics. If you want to keep the job you have now, you have to do some politicking to keep it. And in politics one side breaks open the champagne while the other drys the tears.

Study the jobs ahead

Every company is different but why not do this? Take a sheet of paper and list all of the management jobs from the top down to your level. Go below that if you want to. I suggest you do this for it will give you a picture of what's up above that you can reasonably aim for. Let's say your boss asks, "What is your ambition in the company?" From a study such as this you can name a job or two specifically. And that will be a political advantage because your competition may not have studied those jobs ahead.

Apply some common sense

One executive told me, "I don't have a chance at the top job in my company. That is usually reserved for one of the family. I can shoot at any of the other three top jobs though."

I suggest you look at your company as this man does. Select the job ahead you can aim for. It is up the line some place. It may be far below the real top job, but it is ahead for you. Think of this too, you advance one job at a time. First, you get the job at the level above, then you aim at the level above that. And to move up, even one rung on that ladder, you will have to give up something.

Life is all barter

The other day I watched my nine-year-old grandson and his friend trade cards with the pictures of baseball stars on them. Early in life these boys were learning a principle that will govern their drive for the job ahead should they select business as a career. You have to trade something for something. You give and you get.

I called on a top executive and, as I sat down, heard a rush of footsteps in the hall. "Those guys got the good jobs," he said. "Five o'clock comes and they rush for the elevators. I'd like to go home right now and cut the grass."

I listened to the clatter of the feet on the concrete hallway.

"We worry for them," he went on. "After the five o'clock whistle too."

"But you get paid for it," I stated.

"Yes, it is one of the things we trade for that extra pay."

This is the situation on all management jobs. For managing the man gets more pay, more recognition, more status symbols, but he has to give up something for them. Life in business is all barter. In moving up——

You barter freedom for what you want.

You may ask, "Hold it, what do you mean freedom?"

My executive friend would have liked to go home and cut the grass when that five o'clock whistle blew. But he had to stay on for a meeting that would run for at least an hour. He was trading the freedom of going home when the whistle blew for his position, wasn't he?

As you go up in any organization, you have to

Conform when you would rather not,

Watch what you say,

Listen when you don't want to.

These are three infringements on your freedom and, for some, they are hard to take. You are trading these freedoms for a good opinion of those around and above you. As you go up in the organization, you make many of such trades. Always you are TRADING SOMETHING FOR SOMETHING.

Then consider this thing called pressure.

The pressure gets tougher

As you move up in your company, the pressure gets tougher. The jobs are more difficult to handle. You are getting more pay, you have more authority, you supervise more workers, but more is expected of you. You work harder and you have more headaches. You have to make more decisions, stick out your neck. A number of men below you want your job. A number of men above you may rate you as a menace and may not give you the cooperation they should. All this takes something out of you. You have to be tough to take it. At times it will seem easier to say, "The heck with it," than to come back in the morning and take more of the same.

How much are you willing to give up?

Any business executive has obligations besides his job. Consider this short list.

The wife. As you move up she takes a beating. There are more meetings, more trips away from home that cut into the time you spend with her.

The family. You'll see less of your children. The other night I attended a performance at a children's theater. There were mighty few of the fathers there, not of the executive type anyway. And this is common. You miss family affairs, birthdays, graduations, and such things as that. One executive told me, "My family is the company, I guess. I hardly know my kids."

Social life. One executive put it, "We haven't played bridge with friends for months. I've always had some work to do to keep me busy. It's tough on the wife. Maybe it's tough on me too."

Recreation. Maybe you are a golfer or a fisherman. But, as you advance, you can expect your job to take up more and more of the time you would like to spend at them. If you are lucky, you might get some of your vacation time.

Hobbies. Magazine articles tell you about top men in industry having hobbies such as stamp collecting and woodworking, but ask them how much time they spend at these hobbies. I asked a group of middle-management men in one of my clinics to name their hobbies. Six out of the eighteen said, "Work." I asked the ones who had named hobbies, "How much time do you spend at this hobby of yours?" They admitted that they spent little time at them. One man said, "Let's admit it, Ed, on jobs such as ours we don't have time to properly pursue a hobby."

Give up and get up

These examples help you realize what an executive gives up to get to the top. But does he worry about what he gives up? Perhaps, if you could back him into a corner away from it all, he might admit that he is missing a lot, that he is wasting his life, not having any fun. But most of the men driving for advancement do not think about what they are losing. The other evening I heard a white-collar worker complain because he had to go to a church club meeting, "I have to miss the son's softball game." I thought of the number of executives I knew that perhaps had never gone to a son's softball game.

When the boss sets a meeting for Sunday morning, the climber can't say, "I can't make it. I'm going fishing with the family on Sunday." This is why one man told me, "There is a lot of give and take in this climb to the top. And at times the give seems greater."

There are compensations

The executive who has to give up these things can say, "The wife has her own car because I'm willing to work this hard." That's true, she has. And the family lives in a better house in a better neighborhood, the children go to better schools. They belong to the country club, and they can afford the best of everything. One wife told me, "Jack is working too hard, but, as soon as he gets this promotion, he will be able to ease up." Perhaps that's what Jack told her, but experience does not bear out that theory. When Jack hits that next job, he will work even harder to get the one above that.

Is it worth the effort?

This is the question to ask yourself. Is it worth it? In your case, I mean. Do you want to give up this much? Don't kid yourself into thinking that your case is different, that you don't have to give up. Consider the men who are now on top jobs in your company. What are they giving up? Then ask yourself this important question. "Am I willing to give up that much to get what he has?"

Will your wife stand for it?

Some will and some won't. The average wife likes the advantages that go with success, the extra car, the boat on the lake, the club memberships, the acceptance by the right set, the good schools for the kids, but does she realize what she has to trade for all this? I heard one wife of an executive complain, "He doesn't know he is married to me. He thinks he is married to that company." Your wife took you for better or worse, but will this partial loss of your attention seem worse than she expected? Check through this angle on your drive for that top job before you go all out to make it.

Perhaps you will settle for security

After you have considered these advantages and disadvantages, you might want to settle for a safe job that gives you security. Your loss in that decision is that you may not be working up to your capabilities. Some men can take this and some can't. Your question is, "Can I be happy doing less than I could be doing?"

Management has something to say about this

Your company management may want every employee to make the most out of his talents. Let's say that you select a job you feel you want to stay on. Management may figure that job as a training job for men on their way up. You want this job, and you want to stay on it, but can you? Let's say a promotion is offered you. Because you want your present job you turn down the promotion. Now how do you stand with management? You have gone on record, you don't want advancement. This is a mark against you. Of course, there are jobs you can sit on. And, if you want a spot away from the tumult and the shouting, go after it but keep in mind what you are giving up. And, as I've said before, don't feel that holding that job gets you out of politics. If you want a job with good pay and few headaches, others might want that kind of job too. And so you have to do some politicking to hold on.

Politics is the art of the possible

You hear this quotation a lot in connection with the politics in Washington. The executive suggests to Congress and then gets what is possible to get through the legislative halls.

You find this same situation in company politics. The best politicians aim for the possible. It will pay you to follow that plan.

Your company is different, its personnel is different, the job-ahead situation is different. As you survey your company, you can cross off some jobs up above that are not possible for you because of family connections, seniority, or some other factor that you can't change. Then your education, experience, or willingness to do what it takes to hold the job may keep you from other jobs.

Next, competition for the jobs above may be too tough for you. You may be competing with too many good men. As you study your opportunities to move up in your company, consider what is possible for you, in your situation, in your company. When you have a clear picture of this, shoot for the top, of course, but remember that you may have to settle for the possible. Here is a plan you might try:

1. Explore the idea of getting ahead, one job at a time, to a point as high as you want to go.

2. Realize you have to trade something for something. Study what you give for what you get.

3. Talk the matter over with your wife. Get her on your side.

4. Aim at what's possible for you.

5. Start your campaign.

If this seems like too much effort, you don't have to go through these steps. The company needs some soldiers too. Let's consider another way you might go.

3

Consider the Good Old Bills

You don't have to aim at those jobs up above.

Look around you. There are many men in jobs they do well who have no such ambitions. Let's consider one of these individuals, good old Bill.

Bill is a mighty valuable employee. He has been on his job for twelve years now. He's forty-two, balding, has taken on a bit of weight.

He does a good job.

Everybody likes him, but managers have been brought in over him by five managements. The organization chart calls him a coordinator. "Just a fancy title to keep from giving me more pay," he says. He excuses his years on the same job by saying, "They got to have some privates in an outfit like this." Bill laughs as he says this, but you wonder if he really wants to laugh.

One of Bill's beefs is about his assistant. "They give me a young fellow until I break him in, then they move him on." He doesn't understand that management considers this assistant's job a good training spot. Bill needs the assistant to get the work out. Management assigns an assistant to help train the assistant. The job classification experts say that his job is repetitive. This may be a way of saying that he doesn't have to use his head. But Bill is at the top of his classification, and that is important to Bill because it means that his pay cannot be raised. So Bill is in a bind. But is he really unhappy? Every now and then the man who is beating out his brains looks at one of these Bills and wonders. The striver wonders too if he could be happy with Bill's philosophy, "I don't want to set the world on fire." The life and the pay are not so bad.

Why doesn't Bill move up?

I have worked with a number of these Bills, played with them, socialized with them, liked them, and here are some thoughts on why they did not move up. If you have ambitions to move up in your company, check on how many of these promotion killers are among your habits:

Didn't want to. All through this book, I stress the fact that no law says you have to move up. You can try to stay where you are. I have heard Bills expound on this theory. "Those guys up above have too many headaches and ulcers. Look at me. Sure I got some headaches, but I'm not taking any pills." They say, "Sure the boss makes more dough but he's away most of the time. I'm home with the family every night." The men who get the promotions do have the disadvantages mentioned and others too. So don't pity Bill too much if he really wants to stay where he is. He is doing what he wants to do.

He complains. Bill tells his new assistant, "Don't get too good on this job or you'll be stuck here the rest of your life like I am." What idea does the assistant get from that? That Bill does not like his job, of course, but he also gets the idea that Bill is a complainer. And after he has worked for Bill a few weeks, he finds that Bill is always right, that the people who work with them are all wrong.

He doesn't conform. Bill started this early. He wears his pencil and pen in his outside coat pocket. No executive in the office wears his pencil and pen exposed. You know the type. But that makes no difference to Bill. That is the handiest place for pencils and pen, isn't it?

He doesn't mix. Oh, sure, he belongs to the bowling league because he likes to bowl. But he will have nothing to do with the public speaking class. "There are too many yakkers now," he says. "Why do you guys add to the confusion?" His real reason for not wanting to join the speaking class is that it costs fifteen bucks. But he chooses to shout it down in a way that makes no friends for him.

No strong motivation. He isn't interested in money, power, family, or any of the other factors that cause other men to drive toward the top. He isn't motivated *enough*. Of course, he would like money or power or better things for his family, but he doesn't want them enough to put in the extra licks for them.

Doesn't cooperate. Bill will cooperate with the boys on his bowling team, they're his friends. Any new man gets special attention. "They need a blasting," he says, "to teach them the facts of life." Too often he tells these new people, "What do you think my job is—digging out information for you monkeys?" It's doubtful that this technique makes friends. Too many of the men who have moved up have had the brush-off from Bill.

Wrong attitude. Bill's attitude is defeatist. "It won't work," is his motto. The new advertising theme is for the birds. He explains his failure to move up with, "They like phonies around here and I could never be a phoney." "They let the advertising department spend two hundred thousand dollars and they won't give me a twenty-buck raise."

He's too forthright. He says what he thinks regardless. He asks such questions as, "What knucklehead thought this up?" "I don't beat around the bush," he says. "I tell them and tell them true. Somebody ought to." Perhaps somebody should, but it is not Bill. Bill has never learned to keep his big mouth shut. To think about what he is going to say before he says it.

He takes sides. There are times when everybody has to take sides. But Bill moves in when he doesn't have to. The needlers around the office go to Bill with subjects that will cause him to blow his top. To them it is amusing to see Bill burn. But none of these jokers think of good old Bill as managerial material. He doesn't seem to have balance.

He isn't aware. Bill lacks that quality called awareness. He tells the young fellow who joined the country club because of the contacts he might make, "You can't afford to belong to the country club, you're foolish to spend that dough." This point might be argued, but not with Bill. He'll wear white shoes and a sport shirt to work when even the minor clerks wear dress shirts and ties. At times his clothes look as if he had slept in them. Men up above see this and rate Bill. Of course, he has a right to dress any way he wants to, but how he dresses helps present his image to the king-makers up above.

He doesn't continue to learn. Bill resists the idea that training is a continuous process. He feels he is as smart as any-body, smarter than most. He says, "I got all the education I need for this job and more too." He sees men taking various courses, but this is not for him. He resists the idea that a man's willingness to improve himself helps him get ahead. If he makes mistakes in English, he says, "They know what I mean, don't they?" He reads little besides the headlines, sports pages, and the comics.

Doesn't stick his neck out. Not Bill, he's too smart for that. "You offer a suggestion and you'll find you'll be asked to work out a plan in detail," he says. "That's how they operate around here." And so he has stopped offering suggestions. In meetings he seldom comes up with an idea. He has opinions on others' ideas, knows why they won't work. But Bill doesn't offer any. "Throw out a suggestion and you get your ears slapped back," he says.

Keeps carbon copies. Bill is too smart to be caught in a bind. If the shop doesn't deliver on the 17th and says it didn't know that it should have delivered on the 17th, Bill can come up with a carbon copy of the order that shows he told them. "Keep a carbon copy of everything," he advises. "That way they can't pin the blame on you." Bill misses the point that the main question is the delivery on schedule, not who is to blame.

Not open to suggestions. Bill knows how the job should be done. If a new idea is suggested, he says, "Look, we been doing it this way for years, and it is working OK; the boss is satisfied. Why make a change that may get us all balled up?"

Bill's objective is to keep his nose clean. He is not going to try any ideas that might upset the mail baskets.

Doesn't make decisions. Bill runs to the boss for decisions. "They don't pay me enough to make decisions," he says. The boss asks, "What do you suggest?" Bill says, "I dunno, that's why I came to you." Bill is not going to be reminded later that this was his decision. Later the boss may say, "We made the wrong decision on that." Bill won't let him get away with that. He'll ask, "What do you mean, 'we'? You made that decision."

He is frustrated. Bill beefs quite a bit about his pay. He says, "Why don't they pay a guy enough so that he can belong to the country club. I'd like to play golf on a good course." But it is doubtful that Bill would put up the initiation fee if the company would raise his pay. His record of spending indicates that he wouldn't. He tells the boys that they are crazy for paying five bucks for a brand-name shirt when this Ajax store sells one for two bucks. Bill blames his company for this. He can't afford the five-buck shirts on what they pay him. Others in his wage bracket buy such things but not Bill. Still money is a great subject to complain about.

Do you know good old Bill?

You have this type of Bill in every company. Everybody likes him, laughs at him, and he does a fine job where he is. But can't you see why the kingmakers don't select Bill for that job up above?

He doesn't need all these faults

You've heard the line, "With all your faults I love you still." This applies to Bill, but it is hardly possible that any

Bill would have all of the faults listed. But a lot of Bills **have** three or four or more. And any one of them can scuttle a bright young man, one everybody likes, one that does a good job where he is.

Yet every fault mentioned can be easily corrected if these Bills wanted to correct them. And that wanting to correct the faults and following through to correct them is a part of what we call company politics. For remember this. Bill is doing a good job at his job. These other factors stymie him. Nobody stopped Bill where he is. He put on the brakes himself.

But don't pity Bill

He has a lot of things that the men at the top don't have. His objective is to hang on where he is. He doesn't have to stop, look, and listen before he walks down the hall. He has freedom to

Say what he wants to say

Act as he pleases

Tell off anybody

Be a "no" man

Rail at things he can't change

Bellyache at policies, at management

Criticize anybody and anything

Make the social contacts he wants

Have a full family life

In addition the good job he does gives him a feeling of accomplishment. He is better at his job than anybody.

Bill doesn't have money, power, prestige, sycophants, or two Cadillacs but he has a lot, hasn't he? So don't pity Bill. He does OK by himself.

It's your choice

To be or not to be, that is the question.
To be one of the members of the hierarchy, or
To be a good old Bill.

It is your choice to make. You say you want to move ahead.
Fine, then let's discuss your qualifications.

4

Do You Have What It Takes?

You want to move ahead in your company. That's fine, but do you have what it takes to move ahead? You might answer——

"I have seniority."

"I know more about the business."

"I can run any job in the setup."

All of these were fine qualifications, but in your company do executives get ahead on seniority? Does the power want men with knowledge of the business? Does it want a man with technical skills? If it does, then these qualifications might help you. But to make sure, check.

What does the power want?

You move ahead in your company on what the power in your company wants. You may have other qualities that stamp you as excellent managerial timber, but, if the power doesn't want those qualities, they may be of little use to you. To move ahead in your company your job is to show the power what the power wants. When they look you over, you want them to say, "He's got this, and this, and this, and that's what we need on this job."

First, check what has counted in promotions

Some men have advanced in your company. Why not get what information you can on why they moved up? What helped them to get where they are? What helps them to stay there? Let's say one is a roughneck, another a perfect gentleman. What have these two in common? Analyze the road these men took to advancement. Ask, "Am I on a road that leads to the job ahead or one that leads to a dead end?" Other questions might be, "How do I compare with these men?" "Where am I like them?" "Where do I differ?" You'll find, I'm sure that in almost every case, the man turned in a good job performance on the job he had before he was promoted. Personnel men I interviewed put this "good job" requirement first.

Performance ON YOUR JOB

To get ahead in any company, you take off from a good record on the job you are on. One top executive put it, "Be the top expert on one phase of the business. Get everybody coming to you for advice on that phase and you'll go up fast." Another puts it, "Know the business, know the relationship between departments." A third added, "Bank your future on the way you are performing on the job you have."

Here are some questions you might ask:

How am I doing on my present job?

Good_____Fair_____Poor_____

How does my boss rate me on my present job?

Good_____Fair_____Poor_____

On what parts of my present job am I weak?   _____

_____

What am I doing to improve myself on these weaknesses?

_____

_____

One personnel manager suggested another question to add to this group. "Would you give yourself a raise?"

Talk to your boss

I ask men, "How does your boss rate you on your job?" They answer, "He never says anything. I guess he is satisfied?"

I then ask, "Why not ask him if he is satisfied?"

The questions suggested will give you a pattern for such an approach to your boss. In Chapter 10 I suggest other questions to use in such an interview.

The job well-done is your springboard

Let's assume that, when you approach the boss, he says, "You're doing OK."

Now ask, "How can I do an outstanding job?"

A young factory supervisor told this story. His immediate boss was away on vacation and the big boss told him to clean up a certain section of the factory. The big man said, "That's the dirtiest place in the shop, always has been, and we've never been able to keep it clean." The young man took the two workers available to him, cleaned the section thoroughly, and painted the walls of the section. When the big boss saw what had been done, he asked, "Who told you to paint the walls?"

"It will be easier to keep clean now that it is painted," the young man answered.

"Yeah, I guess you're right," the boss agreed.

When the young man finished telling me about the incident, he asked, "You know what happened, don't you?"

I could have guessed. He got the assignment of cleaning up every section of the plant. "And painting it?" I asked.

"And painting it," he agreed.

But he was on the way up. He had shown the big boss that he could perform. He did what he was told to do and added something, a plus that caught the top man's eye.

Performance gets attention

An executive told about one of his middle-management men who had been passed over in two recent promotions and made an appointment to see him. The visitor asked, "What does a man have to do to get a promotion around here? I've made two written applications to this office and I have heard nothing from either of them. How do I get some consideration?"

The executive said, "Sit down, Tuck."

The applicant sat down. "Now, let me tell you something," the executive went on. "When we get written applications for promotions, we fold them neatly and throw them into this waste basket."

"That's no way to run a railroad," Tuck said.

"Maybe not, but it is our way. What a man says he can do is not nearly as effective as what he shows he can do."

You'll find this attitude in most companies. The best way for a man to show what he can do on a bigger job, is to handle a small job well. Thus one part of that Horatio Alger formula helps any man succeed. Do a good job where you are and you'll attract attention.

What's political about a job well done?

You take care of the political side of the good job by letting others know you are doing a good job, first the boss, then through him the power above him. Let's assume you are doing a good job in your cubbyhole on the second floor. OK, figure out how you can let the power on the floors above know what a good job you are doing. But always channel the information through your boss.

What impression do you broadcast?

In moving about in the company, it pays to think of two images:

a. The image of first impression, and
b. The image of competence.

The image of first impression

A number of small things help in this first impression.

Do you seem alive, alert, intelligent?

Your handshake—does it leave the impression of a wet sock, or is it a grip that makes the other wonder if any bones are broken?

Your face—does it stamp you as a worrier, or a man that thinks things are right with the world?

Your speech—do you make mistakes in English? Talk too fast, slur over words?

Your voice—is it pleasant?

All these contribute to the first impression you make. And you can easily do something about each of them. Suggestions given in the following chapters will help you work on any faults you might have.

First impression can clobber you

You look at me and form an opinion. I look at you and do the same. Of course, further acquaintance can change that first impression, but why not plan to make that first flash as good as you can? A good first impression gets you considered for the job ahead.

The image of competence

This tells others that you have what it takes. You build it by performance on the job, by seeming willing, anxious to learn. Building this image with the power takes time and constant effort. A small boo-boo can wreck years of work. A flop on one job, a bit of bad judgment, an ill-advised wisecrack, a dispute with another executive. In the following pages you'll find hundreds of suggestions for building this image of competence. Without it, you're lost in the competition you'll run into on the way up. So why not ask yourself, "How is my image of competence today and what should I do to make it better?"

How about your health?

Can you take the physical beating that advancement in your company calls for? This depends more on you than on the demands of the job. There is quite a bit of data that shows the executive is not under any greater strain on his health than the factory worker, but, I'm sure, more of them are taking ulcer pills. But you know men who work under constant pressure and don't allow it to bother them at all. Others under less tension go to pieces. In which group are you likely to fall?

Have your physician give you a thorough physical examination. Ask him if there is anything in your physical makeup that might interfere with your moving up in your company. Explain that on the jobs above there will be more work, more worry, more headaches. Get his opinion on whether or not you are so constituted that you can take this. One executive told me, "I don't want a higher job. I want to keep my health. You know it's the only thing I own that is worth anything." If you feel this way, you might not want to try to better yourself.

Check your attitude

The other morning I sat at breakfast in a large hotel with a man who complained continually at the service. He carried on his tirade against the bus boys, waiters, head waiters, and hotel management in front of six men at the table. A man from his company apologized later, "That guy's always belly-aching," he explained. By complaining he told us a lot about the kind of man he was. As you go about your daily work you broadcast news of your attitude in so many ways.

How would your friends rate you? There follows a list of habits that rate you with others. Your friends see more of these habits than management above does. But some of this type of attitude is certain to be observed by the brass. Certain of these habits are helpful and some do you no good at all. Check through the list and see which of these descriptions your friends might apply to you:

An arguer—the man who suggests goes further.

An againster—the man who is "for" does better.

A talker—the fellow who keeps his mouth shut seems wiser.

A changer—the other fellow wants to do things his way sometimes.

A complainer—nobody likes to listen to your beefs.

A critic—who likes to be criticized?

A listener—this man makes friends.

An advisor—get others coming to you for advice and you show one of the qualities of a leader.

A helper—you get a higher rating when you are willing to cooperate.

A courteous individual—a compliment now and then, and a "please" and "thank you" will help you advance.

These ten habits tell others about your attitude toward life and those around you. How much are you using the ones that help you, and the ones that will hold you back? To move up in your company you may have to change some of your habits.

Willingness shows what you have. I once had a boss who repeated this line, "What we need is more men who are willing to work." Willingness is one of your greatest assets in climbing the ladder. Not alone willingness to work, but willingness to do what you are asked to do stamps you with the power and those about you. How willing are you?

Politics in attitude. You may not like to do many of the things you have to do to show the right attitude. Let's say the boss adopts a plan you were against. Now your job is to be enthused about it. You may not like this, you might prefer to stand aside and watch it flop and say, "I knew it would." But instead you work up the reasons why the plan is good and you go out and sell it to your group. It is the same with every one of the points on attitude mentioned. You may not like to follow this course, but it will help you get ahead. And so you get on the bandwagon and show as much enthusiasm as you can.

Can you conform?

How much conformity is asked of you to get ahead in this company? Can you go along with what you are asked to do? Social scientists make a great point of how the worker for the large corporation has to conform to get ahead. But don't think this is confined to the large corporation. In any business a certain amount of conformity is called for. I mentioned the subject of dress. OK, maybe you want to wear yellow shoes with a dark-blue suit. That's your privilege. But if it is not going to help you get to the top in your company, wear the black shoes.

Not long ago we made an automobile trip and spent a number of nights in motels. In the dining room at dinner, Mrs. Hegarty would pick out the salesmen. "How do you know they are salesmen?" I asked.

"They're wearing the uniform," she said.

And the young men were. Dark suits, dark ties, white

shirts. Conformity in dress. A dress perhaps that the sales managers thought would be well accepted by prospective buyers.

Check through the list of things on which conformity is asked from you on your job. Here are some suggestions:

Clothes—can you dress as you are expected to?

Thinking—do you have to feel that all union leaders are crooked?

Political party—do you have to vote Republican, or keep your mouth shut?

College—did you go to the right school, or no school at all?

Country Club—will you have to join the club, even though you would rather not because you can't afford it?

Social life—do you have to play bridge with the right people?

Neighborhood—do you have to live in the same neighborhood as the other executives?

Reading—do you have to read the *Wall Street Journal* and the *Harvard Business Review,* or will that stamp you as dangerously different?

Habits—is it good politics to drink martinis (even though you don't like gin) because the big shots do?

Lodge—do all of the top men wear a pin?

Recreation—do you have to play golf, sail a ship, hunt, fish, when you would rather stay home and rest?

Church—has it paid other executives to shift to the church of the top men?

Many of these requirements may seem silly, a violation of the individual's rights, but to the insider on the way up they can be mighty real. If so, can you go along with those that are? Of course, many nonconformists resist such pressures. I've heard complaints about every one on the list. One fellow puts it, "I can't afford to belong to the country club and so I will not belong."

That's all right, this is a free country. Then another fellow recounts how he borrowed the money from the bank to pay the initiation fee at the country club. He felt it was a good investment.

Most of the things you are asked to do in conforming cost you nothing at all. Many of those listed do not apply in your situation. So why not make a list of the things on which you feel it would be better to conform? Some may be easy for you to follow, others not so simple. But, if conformity will help you succeed, why not go along?

How about education and experience?

A lot has been written about getting ahead on pull and partiality, but no matter what the humorists say, I've seen many men vetoed for consideration for promotion for lack of education or experience. Good men, friends of the brass, but the latter were afraid to take a chance on them. Consider these four types of jobs in a manufacturing company:

Engineering
Manufacturing
Finance
Distribution

Let's assume that you are in one of these departments and are made general manager of the company. Now you have to learn something about the others, don't you? The marketing manager of a division of a company, who was promoted to general manager, told me, "Now, I'm in charge of manufacturing, engineering, and accounting, and I don't know anything about them. In fact, I didn't have too much interest in them." If the manager of any of those other divisions had been made general manager, he would have had a similar problem. Thus it is good to ask, "What further education and experience do I need to move up?"

What do you need?

The other evening I met a young man who was taking accounting at the local college. "Are you in the accounting department of your company?" I asked.

"No, I'm in manufacturing," he said. "But on my next job up, I'll need some accounting. I hate the subject too."

This is the type of training the man on the way up the ladder must think of. If he needs accounting, he does what he can to get it even though he does not like the subject.

Are you a specialist?

In business today we develop specialists. This is one reason why it is difficult to find management men. The fellow is good at his speciality, has no interest in anything else, and has no idea of how to handle people. To offset this, some companies send management men off to universities to study the principles of management.

Now no company assumes that a two-month course in management practices can make a specialist into a manager. But the course gives the promising young executive an idea of those principles of management in which he has shown no interest. It may point out his weaknesses to him; and, if he is willing, he can work toward strengthening those weaknesses.

One job at a time

In most situations you will move up one job at a time. Thus, why not think of getting the training you need one job at a time? What training do you need to fill the job that should be your next logical promotion? Start today getting the training you need for that. Then when you get the promotion, study for the job that is the next step up. As you climb up the ladder, you will be needing more and more training. This brings up the question, "Are you willing to put in the time and effort to get the training you need?"

Check your motivation

You won't do the things mentioned in this chapter unless you have the motivation to do them. You won't conform in dress unless you see how you benefit by conforming. Have you ever tried to check on what motivates you? Here is a list of common motivators of men in business:

Money
Family
Power
Accomplishment
Prestige
Recognition, praise, prestige
Pride in job well done
Fear and worry

Perhaps your chief motivator may not be on the list, but what is it? Whatever motivates you has to be strong enough to keep you driving for what you want in the company.

The other day my eldest grandson came over and asked, "Grandad, you got some work for me to do? I need money."

"What do you need the money for?" I asked.

He wanted a bicycle and he described in detail the type he wanted. That's what I suggest—find out what kind of bicycle you want. Find out what motivates you. Then let your boss know what it is. He knows what he wants out of the company. If he knows what you want, he can use what you want to get a better job out of you.

Take a new look at yourself

Leo Burnett, the head of a Chicago advertising agency that bears his name, puts it this way, "Take a new look at yourself, you may have more stuff than you think." That's what I suggest. And, while you take that look at YOU, try to apply it to what you need to get ahead in your company. You'll find you have this and that and the other, perhaps more than you thought. How does what you have compare with what your company looks for in men it promotes? Then, how can you use what you have to present a better image of you as a man who deserves promotion? Don't hide those plusses, get them out into the open where they can be seen. Here again are the questions to ask to see if you have what it takes to move up:

1. Is your performance on your present job such that you might be noticed for promotion?

2. Do you make a favorable impression on the boss and men above him when you make contact with them?

3. Have you the education and experience that is needed to move up?

4. Will your health stand up under the work and pressure as you move up?

5. Is your attitude such that you would make a good company executive?

6. Can you take all of the conformity that you will be asked to take? Or do you think this is nonsense?

7. Is your motivation strong enough to allow you to take the beating you will have to take?

Now for the types of politics, the political activities, and the politicians that might be bugging you.

5

Know What's Going On

You'll succeed faster in company politics if you

Know the types of politics being played in your company,

Recognize the devices being used in playing this politics, and

Know the individuals behind the political activity.

My suggestion is——

Find out what's going on in your company, and

Determine what you can use and what you have to watch
out for.

Remember your objective is exactly the same as that of
the politicians, and that is——

Favorable contact with the power

The politician wants as much favorable contact with the
power as he can get. He wants the power to keep him in

mind, to remember that he's around. And so he uses various devices to get that notice. If he hears of a party which the boss will attend, he wants an invitation. And even if there isn't the slightest reason why he should be there, he will ask for an invitation. If his boss is presenting a plan to the board, he would like to sit in on the presentation. If there is a story in the company magazine, he'd like to see his name printed as the author, or his picture in one of the photographs. This goes right up the line. Each executive wants more and more contact with the power. One vice-president put it, "A vice-president wants to talk only to other vice-presidents or better." Keep this in mind as you read this chapter.

The politician wants contact with the power. He uses politics and the political devices to get that contact with the power.

Your company has no politics

You may say that your company has no politics or very little of it. But is any of this going on—cliques, feuding, competition for jobs or status, fraternal shennanigans, family influence, and then, of course, party politics? Of course, you have these activities the politician works with——contact, friendships, social activities, church affiliation, recreation, publicity, rumors, leadership, image.

Let's examine how each of these can help or hinder you in your desire to move up in your company:

Cliques. Most of us like to line up in gangs. In a company there may be an old clique to protect the *status quo* to social security. A new one to bump the oldsters off their jobs. Your problem is to get in with the right clique. Each promotion from the clique strengthens its power. Executives say, "We line up with our side, we can't help it." And that is probably true. One man says. "It is better than lining up with no-body." But power shifts, and the man who depends on membership in a clique to help him advance may find himself out of step in a comparatively short time. One top job appointment out of the clique may upset everything.

Departments. This is a clique type of politics that comes naturally. At the company picnic softball game accounting plays shipping, and the girls from accounting scream high and loud for the accounting boys to lay it on. This works back in the office too. And it is natural. You know the people in your department better. When the boss moves up, he recommends one of his assistants for his job. When he wants a new assistant in his new job, he thinks of one man in his old department. One man told me how in his tenure with his company the different presidents had been first, a finance man; second, a manufacturing man; third, a lawyer; fourth, a marketing man. In each case the promotions ran largely to men in the departments the top man came from. The informant stated, "From this it seems that the problem of getting ahead depends to some degree on where you start out." All advice on getting ahead agreed, "Be loyal to your boss and to your department." In most companies, if you are in our department, you are one of us, we're for you, we'll go to bat for you. Be for your boss, your department.

Feuding. This is not for the winner. None of the executives that talked about it felt that it helps the company or the individuals. The heads of two departments are at each other constantly. A good top executive would bring the two together, bump some heads, and tell them to cut it or else. I asked one man, "Why does your big boss allow this?" He answered, "He's keeping the two off him as competition. He knows the feuding will kill them dead as far as advancement is concerned. So he has two less men to worry about." That's politics too, isn't it?

Experts advise on such situations, "Don't commit yourself so completely that you can't back off gracefully."

Competition for jobs. Two or more executives are competing for the job ahead. This is apparent to all and, of course, the subordinates of one executive are for him, while the employees of the other are for the other. The struggle may never reach the stage of open warfare as it does with the feuding executives, but the outsider has to watch what he does or says to see that he doesn't get needlessly involved.

Status. In moving up in a company you run into a continuing struggle for status. The company recognizes this in the status symbols given to the executive as he goes up— larger office, carpet on the floor, venetian blinds. It's apparent in the invitation list to the company meetings or parties. Announce that the top boss will attend your meeting and you'll build up attendance among the executives that want the additional contact with the boss. If one department is throwing a party, the boss checks the list to see who should be invited from the other departments. If it includes everybody on a certain level, fine. An invitation to a man down the line might be used as a reward. For instance, the boss suggests, "Why not invite Elmer who gets out plane reservations, does us a lot of favors?" And so Elmer gets his reward. The boss checking the list, the group flocking to the meeting that the big boss will attend, the invite to Elmer, it's all company politics. What to do? If a man's job rates him to be included, don't forget him. Attend the affair if it will help you.

Fraternal. One factory superintendent was made the membership chairman for his fraternal group. That's right, all of his straw bosses joined up, but fast. And since he ran a large plant, the membership drive was a success. In some companies or departments a man has to be a Mason or a K of C to get considered for promotion. In others a number of the top executives wear lodge pins, and the fellows on the way up keep theirs polished too. Perhaps you belong to the right fraternal group because you like the kind of association you get through it. But, if you don't go for this kind of thing, don't offer any negative opinions on it. Word of such an attitude gets around. If a fraternal connection can help you, take advantage of it. But remember, it can only be a small plus.

Mergers. This is a mess that nobody can figure. The press release says, "Business will be handled just as it was in the past, no change in policies, no change in personnel." But in the meantime there is immediate movement among the executives for position. A check is made on the policy of the new power in former mergers. Some executives make contacts with the new power, or employees of the new owners. Rumors come from nowhere. Some men decide quickly to get out while the getting is good. The confusion that was standard becomes worse. All know that the policy of no changes will hold for a time, but then they expect the outsiders to move in. One executive advised, "Sit tight and see what happens. You might wind up better. And, if they have to separate you, you're probably entitled to some severance allowance." Another told me, "I've been clobbered in two mergers, but now on this third one, I've hit the jackpot."

Thus the merger may be good or bad for any individual. But there is one consolation. Another company considering you for a job won't think your being ousted because of a merger as a liability. And all the political skill you learned on this job will help you on the next.

Family. Last year convention speakers were using the story about the young man who had been made a vice-president of a large company. The president called him into the office and said, "It's quite an achievement to be made a vice-president of this company at the age of twenty-five. What have you got to say to the president about that?"

"Thanks," the young man said.

"Thanks, what?" the president asked.

"Thanks, Dad."

Audiences laughed. But perhaps the young man did not have too much to laugh at. It may be tougher to work for the old man than to work for an outsider. Perhaps you have known young men like this on jobs with good title, good pay, but frustration, looking for something else without the title or the high pay, but with more freedom. It's the same if Uncle Bert got you the job. He's got influence and you're in. Perhaps you are doing the best ever done in that job, the salary increases are coming regularly and you're moving up. But there's Uncle Bert. You can't get him out of your mind. In large corporations the son who follows his father into the business may hear, "If you're half the man your dad was, you'll do well here." Now what does the young fellow do? He should smack the man right in the kisser, but he doesn't, he burns. Family can affect a man in two ways. If you are not connected, there may be certain jobs you can't get, but all of the other top jobs are open to you. If you are connected, you may have to work harder to make your way up. The old man may still think of you as his teen-age son, remembering the boo-boos you pulled in the past.

Party politics. This can make a capable man seem an outsider. One executive told me about the pressure put on him to contribute to the Republican party. His boss was the local fund-raising chairman and all kinds of pressure was put on him to give one hundred bucks. He reported they told him, "That's the amount set up for men in your kind of job." The big boss didn't approach him. He sent one of the assistant managers. The executive went to the boss. He told him that he did not want to contribute to the Republicans, that he was a Democrat but, because the big boss was on the spot trying to make a record as a fund-raiser, he would give the one hundred bucks. Did this action help or hinder the executive? He didn't know. "It sets me apart," he said. "It may or may not help me." The big boss might have said, "Ham, if you feel that way about it, give the one hundred bucks to your party and I'll call off my dogs here. We may need some friends on the other side."

Unless he is with the dominant group, the company politician does not declare himself. He keeps his mouth shut. One told me, "I go along with them, give them the dough; but, when I'm in that voting booth, I do what I want."

There are other types of politics

The types of company politics listed are the ones that you are most likely to run into. In checking for these types in your company, you'll find others that might affect you. There follow short descriptions of many of the political devices the company politician uses to further his ends.

Contacts. Let's say you came from the president's home town, or went to his school, or belonged to his fraternity. It may not be too easy to capitalize on this, but it is a plus. You might mention the fact when you meet him at one of the company parties. If personnel brings your file to him when a promotion is up, those facts stand out. There is no sense in it perhaps, you shouldn't be any better on the job because of those accidents, but the record is there and it counts. Contacts below help too. You worked with Pete who runs shipping that first summer you were on the job and now Pete will do anything to get your shipments out for you. Thus such contacts help you make a better showing on your job. The company politician knows this and he keeps alive his old contacts and makes as many new contacts as he can.

Friendship. The boys you went to school with, your buddies, your pals, they too will do what they can to help you move up. The company politician knows he should keep those friends, show an interest in them, and make other friends just as he made them.

But friendship can work for and against you. Politicians in business try to make friends of the right kind, ones that can help. They avoid friends that will hurt them. If you associate with the bright young men on their way up, it is natural to assume that you are on your way up. If you are one of the gang that stops each evening at the bar and grill on the corner for a quick snort before you start for home, you may be rated as something else. There's an old saying, "Tell me about a man's friends and I'll tell you about him."

The good politician selects friends that have similar ambitions to his, that are interested in knowing more about the business and in training themselves to get ahead.

Social activities. Do the people you run with outside office hours help you advance in the company? The politician picks his social companions with a thought of how much they can help him. Of course, the climber is striving to socialize with those above his level. It may be more fun to run with the group at his level, but he can make more capital for advancement by aiming a bit higher. You may disapprove of this. But you will see much of it. And it might pay you to do some of it yourself. The invitation to the vice-president's cookout, even though you have to keep the fire going, is the right kind of contact, isn't it?

Church affiliation. This may not make much difference in the large city where the workers live in different suburbs and few know which church you attend or whether or not you attend at all. But in the small town, the church you belong to has some effect. I heard an outside consultant advise a man who was being considered for a job, "When you get into this town you had better join a church." The applicant said, "No, I won't join a church. I don't belong to one now and I'm not going to join one." The consultant had no particular church in mind. He wanted the new man to join a church because everybody in the company belonged to some church and, if the new man did not belong to one, he would be thought different. "In my town," one executive reported, "when we bring a new man in, it seems he and his wife try to find out who goes to which church and in so many cases they select the one that the big shots attend." Such a man feels that his selection will give him a connection with the top men. He feels the top people might say, "He must be OK, he goes to our church." You may say, "This is not right." It isn't, of course. If you take your creed seriously and don't want to or can't use it to help you advance, don't laugh at the ones who do. They are your competition.

Recreation. The gang you play with, sail, bowl, softball, golf with, these men are a part of your political life. A young man who had been a member of the golf team at his college moved into one company I worked for and in a short time he was playing golf with the higher executives. They didn't play the low handicap game he did, but they liked to have the good golfer with them. The young man moved up faster because of his golfing skill. I once had a job to fill and one of my assistants recommended a fellow who worked in the factory. "Where did you meet this man?" I asked. "He is on our bowling team," my associate said. The contact on the bowling team got the man the chance at the job. The man worked out well too, and improved his lot quite a bit through the years.

This type of thing is always happening in business, and you see it every day about you. The fellow who plays gin with the boss at noon hour may tell him things too. Or hear things that he can use. Play at your favorite sport with a man and he knows you better and is inclined to think of you when he needs help.

The company politician takes advantage of those activities that will help him. If the boss likes fly-fishing, perhaps he will take up fly-fishing.

Publicity. If one of the managers up above has a story about his work in the company magazine, check to determine what is the objective. Is he trying to boost himself, or is the author's boss behind all this? Some executives try to hog all the publicity about the work of the department. The politician who knows this suggests other ways his boss can get publicity.

Publicity does help the executive advance, for the power reads what is printed in the company magazine, or in the local newspapers.

Rumors. If you hear a lot of rumors about the company and its intentions, the company politicians may be at work. Ask the question, "What's the purpose of such a rumor?" If you feel that a rumor is harmful to the company, ask, "who will this rumor help?" If it disturbs you, ask, "Was this told to me to disturb me?" Remember any political rumor may be aimed directly at you.

Leadership. You had this in high school. Some fellow was the president of one activity, another a leader in a second activity. In school you may have been indifferent to this, but in your company similar activities impress the power. The man who organizes the public speaking class is attracting attention to his leadership. The one who organizes the class in management practices shows that he wants to be a better manager. This is a type of political activity that management encourages, and it pays most men who want to advance to join such groups, even lead them. Of course, it is good politics to ask the advice of your boss, get his suggestions before you go off on any such project.

Image. Image is a political asset or liability. It helps others form an opinion of you, those above and those below. If you look capable, the power may ask about you. In many companies you'll find the better jobs going to men who present the best image. Image doesn't help one bit in getting your job done. But it does bring notice to you and so it is a political plus. Check the men about you and see which of them work hardest at presenting the image of capability that helps the executive advance.

Where's the dirty politics?

I have purposely passed up many of the types of politics and political devices that have come up in my interviews, such things as promoting of a man upstairs to get him out of the way, putting him on a nonproductive, blind-alley job where he will waste away or quit, using his wife's unfitness to keep him out of the job, framing him by sending carbon copies of his letters to the wrong people, withholding cooperation so that he fails in what he is trying to do. There are such goings on and plenty of them, according to my informants, but I am not going to write about them. And don't go looking for them. You have a big enough job searching for the clean politics that is being played in your department and in your company. Check on what is going on, and remember——

1. The object of all company politics is to curry favor with the power, starting with your boss and then going upward through him.

2. It pays to know the types of politics being played in your company so that you can take advantage of them.

3. If you can recognize the political devices being used, you won't be scuttled by an activity carried on under your nose.

4. If you know the politicians, you are in a better position to handle them instead of allowing them to make a patsy out of you.

Now let's discuss how men influence your future.

6

Men Determine Your Future

A company is men.

Its success is dependent on men.

Your success is dependent on men.

You may work for a fine company, a company that has a product in great demand. But if the company doesn't have the manpower to realize its prospects, it's not going to offer you the future that it should. Three groups of men determine how far you can go in any company:

First, your competition, the others striving to get ahead.

Second, your boss, and

Third, the power above your boss.

How does your company rate on these men, comers, managers, leaders?

Let's be selfish for a minute

Let's forget what the company wants from you and take a look at what you want from the company. You want a job in a good company, operating in a good business, one that is making a profit, and that has prospects for growth and expansion. You check with that, don't you? Then why not analyze the men who run your company with relation to their ability to run the company in such a way that it will produce these benefits for you? I suggest this check because there are other companies that can offer you all you want. Those companies are looking for men who want to get ahead. So why waste your time in a company that can't offer what you want?

You might start your check with these questions:

Start with the top men

Do they accept new ideas or do they run from them? Do they keep up with changes in the industry? Is there any deadwood in these top jobs, any men who should have been retired years ago? Do these aged men have too much to say about how things are run? Is the top man a part-time worker, off in Florida most of the year? Analyze these men just as they would analyze you if you were an applicant for a job. Then check the board of directors man by man. Why is each on the board? To help operate the company or for what he can get out of the company? Don't say these men are fine people to work for, ask, "Are they building a better job for me?"

What's the company program?

This reflects management thinking. Does it work from day to day, have a program of expansion, or is it cutting down?

Are the men at the top pushing this program? Is the program dictated by outsiders? Is the program realistic, one over which you can enthuse? Is the refusal to modernize due to a bull-headed stubbornness of top men who feel safe in their jobs as things are now? Do these men fear even the smallest change? Is management willing to spend a dollar to make two? Are they willing to put out the extra work needed to expand the company?

How about age?

Does the management retire men at sixty-five or allow them to retire when they want to? Allowing the older man to stay on keeps a job closed to the younger man. How can this affect you? Does this policy affect the business of the company? Most older men will argue that the company needs the experience, but does it? Does the company refuse to hire executives over a certain age? How close are you to that age?

Next middle management

One company president said, "We're weak in middle management!" My question was, "Are you doing something about it?" If the men on the job above you are weak, is the brass trying to do something about it? Check on the last promotions into this group. Do these men show promise or are they just hole fillers? Does the company have a training plan to equip men for these middle-management jobs? If this group continues weak, perhaps management doesn't know it's weak, or doesn't know how to correct the condition. This situation may be of help to you if you can outperform men on such jobs. But what is it doing to your future?

How about the business and the industry?

Get all of the data you can on the business and the industry. Perhaps the company makes and distributes Whatsis and the world is not using as many Whatsis as it once did. But management can't see this, and keeps on turning out Whatsis without shifting emphasis to other products that the public seems to want. Is the industry growing or standing still, getting a smaller or greater share of the consumer dollar?

How about competition?

Does it seem more progressive, more alert to changes in customer demand, willing to change its product to meet public demand? Is it taking business away from your company? What's the reason for this? Is your company losing position in the business?

How about company honesty?

Can you go along with the company's methods of treating customers, its advertising claims? Its treatment of the help? All of these reflect the men in power in the company. If management is not honest with the public and the distribution, why should it be honest with you?

What's the pay scale?

One president told me that his company's pay compared well to the industry. I checked with executives and found this was not so. "But the old man says we're paying enough," one vice-president told me. Pay can reduce the quality of your company's manpower, particularly in the middle-management group.

Usually the pay scale reflects the thinking of the top brass. One executive said, "If you don't pay, you don't get."

Does the company lose good men?

One executive told me that his company had four general managers in three years. Why? If your company is losing good men, try to find out why. Don't be satisfied with an explanation that the new job doubled his salary. Ask, "Were there other reasons?" Talk to men who are leaving. Wish them luck on the new job and ask a few questions about why they are leaving. You want to avoid spending your time to advance so far and then have to leave because your progress is stymied by some condition that you can foresee right now.

Not all favorable answers

The answers to all of these questions won't be favorable. No job could be quite that good. But do your answers show that the manpower in your company is adequate to help you get what you want? That's what you want to know. There is no sense in succeeding in company politics if you are in the wrong spot to reap the reward. Of course there are other questions you can apply to the brass in your company. But in doing any such analysis, be selfish about it. Ask yourself, "How does this affect my future?"

Factors on which you can rate any executive

In the following you'll find listed some factors on which you can rate any executive, your boss, those above him, and those at your level and below. With each factor there are some notes to indicate what to include in these ratings.

The physical. How old is he, how big, what kind of personality? What's his image in the company?

Education. Is it adequate for the job he has, for the jobs above he might be asked to take? Is he adding to it?

Experience. What has he done, how long has he been at it?

Past record. Has he done well on his past jobs? Is he known for doing a good job wherever he is?

Health. Is this adequate for the job he holds? Will it stand up under the pressure of the jobs ahead? Does it give him the drive he needs?

Ability. Is he doing a good job, fair job, or outstanding job where he is?

Attitude. Is he for the company and its policies? Optimist, pessimist, or in between?

Conformity. Does he act like a company man? Is he an individual, a radical, a loner?

Human relations. Does he get along well with his help and those around him?

Honesty, integrity, character. Can you trust him? Is he the type of individual you would pick for a model?

Sponsorship. Who is behind him? Who put him where he is, who is pushing him ahead?

Ambition. What does he want to make out of himself? Does he want to go up or is he content where he is?

Go ahead, try to rate somebody

How do you feel that the boss rates on these factors, or the fellow across the desk from you? Try to rate one of them or both. These factors are used by the power when they rate men for promotion in business. You have to do some of this rating in any supervisory job. You rate the men that work for you, the ones you hire, the ones you fire. All through the following pages you are asked to rate men on how they can help you get ahead. So why not try rating a few specimens. For remember this:

1. The men in your company help you build a future.

2. If your company has the manpower to go ahead, you can go ahead.

3. If your company does not have the manpower, you might have to look elsewhere for a company that can offer you what you want.

4. Be selfish about this analysis. Why play politics where politicking will do you no good.

If this indicates that success in company politics means work, I agree, but it pays off well. Now we'll talk about how the men above, below, and around you influence your future.

part **2**

How to Move Ahead or Hang On

Let's say you decide to move up in your company, or to hang on to the soft job you like. To accomplish either objective you will be called upon to engage in politics with——
Your competition
Your boss
The power above your boss
Associates, and
Employees who work for you
Men who have successfully played company politics gave me the suggestions outlined in the following chapters. These tips can help you keep the job you have, get you the next promotion, and each of the succeeding promotions as you move ahead.

7

Analyze Your Competition

You are not alone in your ambition to get to a job ahead. Others have this idea too.

Have you ever taken a good look at those others?

Have you ever made a count of the jobs ahead to which you and those others can aspire?

It will pay you to do this, just as the top man in your company does it. This kingmaker, the man who makes the final decision on who moves up, knows he will have jobs available up above. To fill these jobs when they come up he has a manpower pool of which you and these others are a part. So why not check on what he has in men and jobs? It will show you what you can reasonably expect.

How to analyze competition

Follow these three steps in this analysis:

First, list the jobs available,

Second, list the men available, and

Third, analyze the men and their fitness for the jobs ahead.

I am not suggesting that you do this in ten minutes or on the back of an envelope. It is an important study for a fellow who wants to succeed in company politics and should take some time.

First, list the jobs

Use the organization chart to make this list. If there is no organization chart available, make up one of your own. List all jobs above your level. You might include your level if some of the jobs are better than others and it is company practice to move men around at this one level.

Second, list the men available

In making the list of men, I suggest you list those above you, those at your level, and the comers below you.

Those above you. You have to list these people, for they are your competition too. They have to move up or move out before there is a higher job for you to move into.

Those at your level. These are your immediate competition. You have to outscore them to make the impression that gets you the big chance. These fellows are competitors, but they can also be allies. While you are at your present level, they can help you and you can help them. This may also be true as you advance up through levels immediately above yours.

The comers below you. List these too, for some of them may have the ability to travel up faster than you or some of the others at your level.

Third, analyze the men and their fitness for the jobs ahead

Now that you have listed the men, you can scratch off a number of them as competition. Leave on the list those that have ambition comparable to yours. Some, of course, will be content to be good old Bills. Cross them off. Now analyze those left on the list of the factors in Chapter 6. A quick check of the factors will take some others off your list.

Put each through your wringer. In Chapter 4 I suggested a number of checks to make on yourself to see if you had what it takes. Well, put these names on your list through those same tests. There follow suggestions to help you in this analysis. Any time you spend on this analysis of others is valuable to you because the higher you go up in management the more rating you will have to do. Thus the time spent on rating and analysis is good management training.

Analyze the image of each. After a bit of practice you'll get good at this. Buster is a tall guy, good looking, he oughta be in the movies. Looks good at first sight, but are these looks a front? What's he got inside? Digger is a short fellow, a pusher. You think he is too much of a pusher. Small men usually are. Will that pushing scare his boss and the higher-ups? You can't help but have opinions. And opinions are politics. You think that Junker is a smart fellow because he never opens his mouth to voice an opinion. Ever consider that he might be stupid? That silence may be a part of the wise-man image he is trying to create. Give these fellows the same close scrutiny that you gave yourself. Make notes of what they got that you haven't got. Rate them—good—fair—average—poor.

Does he give good reasons when he answers questions?

When he brings you a problem, does he suggest a solution?

You may like the fellow, he may have the appearance, but dig a bit deeper.

What has each done? Not long ago I told an executive that one of his men had a master's degree in business from Northwestern. He said, "I didn't know that, and we're looking for a man with that background for a research project." This type of information is important to the boss, and it is important to you in your check of your competition. I'd suggest you chart the career of each man at your level. You say you don't know about it. Well, ask him. Any man is glad to tell you about the work he has done. This history gives you some ideas about how much competition he will be. If the job above calls for a man with factory experience and this competitor has it, he has a better chance at the job. Tenure too is important. A man who has been with the company only one year is not so likely to be promoted as one of comparable ability that has been with the company three years.

What records has he made? Some of your competition will have made fine records. Let's say that one man at your level has been running a department that has increased its profit more than any other in the company. With the management that fellow may be the white-haired boy. OK, take this into consideration. Another may be a cost cutter, a third an expert on automation, a fourth may be running his department with half the payroll. You get such information in conversation. I asked one friend how his company came to make him a vice-president. "It's mainly luck, Ed," he said. "I was in charge of the department that made the largest percentage of profit." Now luck may have had some effect on the promotion, but management didn't choose him because he was lucky. It saw that profit record. If the man could make a profit record in one department, he might do the same in the four new departments that were assigned to him.

Last night in the newspaper I read of a works engineer in a local plant who had made over two hundred acceptable suggestions on cost cutting in the factory. Don't you think that management has its eye on that fellow for possible promotion?

Let's say as the kingmaker you have a decision to make between two men for a promotion. One is the best speech maker in the company. The second is a profit maker. Which would you choose? In most cases it would be the profit maker. Speeches are fine, but the company pays dividends with profits. So note any records competition has made. Ask yourself, "What records has this man made?"

What does he read? This is a clue to the type of competition a man will be. Does he say, "I get so much company crap to read that I have no time for outside reading?" Give him a plus if he reads one or more of the financial papers and the trade magazines. This again is job reading. If he reads only the comics and the sports pages, he might not be too much competition. What books does he read? By reading books he increases his production of ideas, and those ideas will help him move up to the top. Thus the competitor who reads books will be tougher competition for you.

Consider the background of the top men. In analyzing competition, consider the background of the kingmakers. In the newspaper I read a story stating that the head of the engineering department was made president of the company. Now this would be a boost for the engineers and, if it happened in your company, it makes the engineer on your level a tougher competitor for only one reason—the new president is likely to know him better. One personnel man wrote me, "Originally my company was run by the sales department, then during the depression years finance took over, next a manufacturing man took over, and now it is nearer a combination. When finance was in, most promotions went to financial men. Since production took over more production men get the better jobs. Today, as I analyze the promotions, I note that marketing men seem to be moving faster toward the top."

Another personnel man said, "Up until four years ago our top men were all factory men. Then we changed to a marketing man at the top. Our business has more than doubled in those four years." The background of the top man may have a lot to do with what competitor moves up. If the company is large, the top man finds it quite difficult to know the promotable men in all of the departments.

I suggest this background study because it can affect your future. The top man knows the men from his side of the business, he understands their work. If he has to choose between two men of equal ability, he'll probably select the one whose work he can better appraise.

You may call this politics. The boss promoted the man because he knows him. Well, what would you do in a similar case?

How about relatives? Is this company of yours a family company? If so, "How far up can you go?" One sales manager I worked with on some meetings told me that he had quit his job. "I thought you had a good thing there," I stated.

"I did," he said, "but what was my future? I didn't want to be a number-two man to Junior."

If you are in a company that is a family company, try to analyze how far you can go in such a setup. Junior doesn't have to be the smartest fellow in the world to succeed to the father's job.

You'll find these types

In making this list you'll find these types:

Top men. These cause you to feel that they have possibilities for growth.

Average. These in your opinion will never set the world on fire. They may not want to, or they may be too slow to catch on.

Below average. These are destined to be the privates in the ranks, who don't want to take responsibility, or who shouldn't be given it.

Yes–men. The kind of men that try to figure out what the boss wants before they commit themselves. Does this help him with the boss?

The negatives. These are doubtful that any plan will work, that assert it might be better if we left things as they are, worshipers of the *status quo.* Is this because the boss thinks this way?

The dedicated. These think the company can do no wrong, that management can't, that think any criticism is heresy. Does this help?

The court jesters. These are always ready with the wise-crack no matter how serious the subject. Assets at department parties, but they do give management the impression that they are not too serious about the business.

Check your list against these classifications

Try to classify the names on your list into classifications given. You can probably cut off the average and below aver-

age, the yes–men, the negatives, the court jesters. Or could
you in your company? Perhaps average men do well.

How to tell a comer

I've suggested you list the comers below you. OK, how do
you pick a comer? Here are some of the types of questions to
ask about him.

Does he present a good image?

Do you know his ambitions?

Does he talk sense?

Does he seem logical in his thinking?

Does he button up his jobs?

Does he seem willing?

Stick to your own division

If you work for a large corporation with a number of
divisions, many of the top jobs are probably staff jobs at a
remote headquarters. The suggestions I give here apply
mainly to the competition in your own division. As a rule
the business of the different divisions is so varied in nature
that it is difficult for a man in another division to understand
the business of the other divisions. Thus don't burden yourself with trying to figure the competition in other divisions.
Stick to your own bailiwick. There are jobs up ahead, aren't
there? It is these boys at home that you are competing with
now.

How many are competition?

Perhaps you started with a list of ten possibles. Your checks
have cut it to five or six, or perhaps two or three. Do you
feel you have an equal chance with these men remaining on

the list? You do? Fine, then what do you do next? Here are some suggestions on

How to handle your competition

You can take a tip from good sales practice here. Don't knock it. The answers I got in my survey suggest—— (1) know it; (2) respect it; (3) understand it, and (4) cooperate with it.

1. *Know it.* You have done that with the checks suggested. You have checked out the men that you feel will not go up. You have put your finger on those that you feel have what it takes to advance. With this knowledge you are in a better position than if you had just made a list with guesswork. You are not figuring Chuck, who looks like a movie star, as a competitor for you have analyzed Chuck and found that, behind those looks, he does not have what it takes. You have eliminated those that don't have the desire or the willingness. Here is the political advantage of the analysis of competition. I doubt that any other man on your level in your company has done this. Thus you are better-informed. You know who your competition is. The others may have never thought of it. Most men don't. They go along doing their jobs from day to day without thinking about other moves on the checkerboard that may affect them. Since you know your competition you can watch it.

2. *Respect it.* You have checked out this competition, you have some idea of its strengths and weaknesses. Why shouldn't you respect it. The baseball pitcher says, "Any joker up there with a bat in his hand is a potential hitter." Adopt this attitude toward all competition. Ambrose may lisp, but he's got so much on the ball that his speech impediment may not

handicap him at all. Speak well of your competitors; say "Pete has a lot on the ball." Listen to their ideas. Show interest in them. Ask for their opinions. Ask what they read and discuss their reading habits. Ask, "When do you find time to read?" If the other fellow has been taken by an idea on time saving he read about, he'll be glad to discuss it with you. You can learn a lot from this competition if you will take the time to learn. But respect it, respect its work, its ideas, its ambitions.

3. *Understand it.* To understand a man you do not have to agree with all he says or does. But, if you understand him, you have a better chance of getting along with him, preventing friction or bickering. We know that the best way to understand a man is to talk to him, listen to him, ask him questions. Men tell me, "I don't think that guy likes me." I ask, "What is that man's main interest?" After we have agreed on this, I suggest that the complainer go and ask the man some questions about the man's interest. Invariably the complainer comes back and admits, "I was wrong about that fellow. He hasn't got anything against me." Use this idea with your competition. If the man recognizes you as competition (and he may have given no thought to this), he may act distant to you. Talk to him and you both get a better idea of the other fellow. Confer with him as often as practicable, listen while he opens up and discusses his ideas. Ask him questions that show you are interested. You'll find that he will do the same to you. If a man gets along great with his help, but not with anybody else, you can wonder about it from afar but, if you talk to him, you come closer to understanding why he is that way.

4. *Cooperate with it.* You no doubt have run into situations in companies where one department head will not work with another department head. The men are competitors for that job ahead and are killing their chances of getting it. When I mentioned this to one such head, the fellow said, "Well at least that other so-and-so won't either." What do the ones who know of this feud think of the antagonists? They can't have a high opinion of them, can they? I had one president tell me, "I've got to get those two guys and bump their heads together." The sooner the better you'd agree, wouldn't you? The constant bickering hurts both men's chances and it slows the flow of work too.

Don't feud with your competition, work with it. One wag puts it, "You had better. You never know who will be your next boss." Get the thought that, while this man is a competitor, he can also be an ally. One personnel man advises, "Find men with comparable interest and form or join cliques." We think of the clique as wrong. The fellows who play poker on Friday night at the Elks are one kind of clique, the boys who are taking a course in management practices are another. When I talked about this clique idea at a management class, one of the men asked, "That's what we're doing here, isn't it?" It was, and it was a clique activity that all agreed was good for the company.

What can you see ahead?

One step in the formula at the start of the chapter was, "List The Jobs Ahead." As you consider the men available, also take into account the jobs available.

Let's say in your company you have two jobs ahead and ten men working for them. That's quite different from the company that has the two jobs and three men working for them. Consider this "men and jobs" angle as it applies to your situation in your company.

One man told me, "There are three men in my department

with about my ability. We can't all go up. I might do better in a department where they don't have so much talent."

If you see this situation, talk to your immediate boss about it. You gain in two ways by this talk: first, there may be some changes in the works that you do not know about. Perhaps some of that competition is being transferred. Second, by talking to the boss, if conditions are as you think, you will have your boss helping you move to a different department. Before you talk to your boss, study the personnel in other departments and select one in which there is no logjam up ahead. You can then say, "I'd like to transfer to B department." If you are to get ahead, it is better to be in a spot where you don't have to move tough competition out of the way before you can advance.

Don't fear competition

Welcome it. William Feather says, "Competition reduces all of us to size." It also keeps us on the ball too. Let's say that the boss has one assistant. It has been policy that, when the boss moves up, his assistant gets the job. Does that assistant have as much incentive to work for that job as he would if the boss has two assistants, about equal in what it takes? You know he doesn't. It is for this reason that any competition you have helps you. To gain recognition you have to outperform the others.

Work under cover

Here is another bit of political advice, "Don't blab about this survey of yours." Nobody else will be doing it, and those you tell may think of you as a nut or something. Keep the idea and your conclusions under cover. You did this for your information, in the interest of your advancement. Your analysis can't help anyone else, so don't burden them with it.

Here is your plan to check on competition

1. List the jobs ahead.
2. List the men available.
3. Analyze the men and their fitness for the top jobs.
4. Analyze the outside factors that might determine promotion.
5. Come up with a list of competitors.
6. Work with competition.

Now that you have checked this far, let's look at another factor that has to do with promotion.

8

Find the Power and Impress It

Find the power in your company.

You say that is easy. "It's the president. He makes all the final decisions on promotions." Fine, but who hands the names up to the president?

Let's say that your company has a president, an executive vice-president and a vice-president and treasurer. Is one of the trio the kingmaker or is it a joint operation? These are things you should know.

The other day a friend told me of a company whose chairman of the board was ninety years of age and the president eighty-two. The two played golf three times each week. My thought was, "Who's minding the store?" Do you think that those two old codgers are the kingmakers in that company? My friend says they are, but I doubt it.

I met a member of the Young President's Club the other

day. At thirty-four he was president of his company. I asked him, "Who decides on promotion in your company?" He said, "I started this company five years ago. In those early days I did all that myself. Today I have some help." An employee in that company has to locate that help.

Why find the power?

Perhaps it is the fellow you pay no attention to. But if you know he is it, you'll show a bit of interest in him, won't you? There may be little sense in playing up to men who appear to be the works, but aren't. One executive told me, "I'm in the jay bird's seat. I play golf with the president of the company every weekend." He is sitting pretty if the president is the kingmaker, but supposing the president has little say. As I study the management of various companies, I find that in many of them the organization chart leads you astray. Thus I say, find the power, the real power, the ones that are the kingmakers. These men can bring your name before the mighty.

Start in the right place

I put it rather strong when I said that there may be no sense in playing up to those who are not the works, for it is well to leave a good impression with everybody. But in any company, in any situation, the first man to impress is your immediate boss. If he doesn't feel that you are a comer, you are not going to get very far. Impress him, and some of that impression will be passed on to his boss. That brings news of you further up the ladder. Today the most important power for you is your immediate boss. Your day-to-day assignment is to impress him. Do all the things the storybook maxims advise, do a good job, keep your nose clean, show you are interested, willing, loyal. But do a bit of checking too.

Study your department

The power that affects you right now is the power in your department. Let's assume that your department is a part of a division of the company. Now each of these units has a seat of power. But right now, the power you are most interested in is in your department. It should be easy for you to determine where it is for you know your department better than any other unit in the company. So ask yourself, "Who is the power here?"

How to find the power in your company

Last week, as an executive showed me the organization chart of his company, he said, "The chairman and president spend about six months every year in Florida. The vice-president and the treasurer really run the company." Somebody else had to be the kingmaker during the time the top men were off fishing and golfing and sunning themselves. Of course, they were probably asked to approve any moves. But the moves were made by the men who stayed home to watch the cash register. How do you find the real power then? Here are some suggestions:

Ask questions. You can ask questions on this subject that indicate you want to know something that is none of your business. You ask, "Who is the kingmaker here?" The listener might think, "Why does he want to know that?" But let's say you ask, "How does Mr. Bjax fit into this picture?" Ask such questions of workers at your level. Ask them at lunch, at coffee breaks, in the car coming to work. Think out the questions you ask. Ask more than one person the same question. One man's answer may be discolored by his feelings for Mr. B.

In some companies the personnel practice is to designate a number-two man in each department. This man would take over if the number-one man was moved out. Find out if you can who this number-two man is. If there is no such designation in your company procedure, ask questions to find out who is likely to succeed your boss in case he moves up. Again you might get conflicting answers. But the names give you suggestions as to the men you should impress.

Discuss with your boss. He might ask, "Why do you want to know?" Tell him, "We want to show that the department is on the ball, don't we?" He can't object to that. If he agrees that the department wants to make an impression with its service and its record, ask, "Who is it most important to impress?" If he ever says, "You can't do that because it might offend Joe Whosis." Ask, "Why shouldn't we offend him?" The other night I heard an executive say, "The damned accountants are running our company now. We don't have money enough to put out even the simplest instructions." That statement tells you something, doesn't it? In discussing such matters with the boss you tell him that you are ambitious, that you want to get ahead, that you want the right people pulling for you. If you are doing a good job for him, he can't help but admire you for this.

Talk to old-timers. You have a number of people in the department who have been around for a long time. Good old Allie who sits there in the corner office, you've seen the boss sit down and talk to him. Someone tells you they went to school together. You've seen executives from upstairs do the same. Talk to old Allie and others like him. Let them tell you how it was in the old days, give you some of the history of the business and the company. Ask them about individuals. He may tell you that a young man you think is a comer is just an errand boy for someone upstairs. Check this, of course, but Allie has seen a lot of errand boys, and he is likely to know another when he sees him. He may tell you, "That fellow is never going to be satisfied until he gets to the top." That's a tip on competition, isn't it? Allie has seen them come and go. He knows the politics of the company from away back. Listen to him, show an interest in what he says. He can help you understand what the shooting is for.

Talk to associates. One of your executives gets a promotion. Ask your associates, "Why do you think he got the job?" You'll hear such reasons as, "He was next in line." That is a logical explanation. But let's say the man was brought in from another department. "Why?" You'll get such answers as, "He did a good job where he was." Fine, but how did the word get up to the kingmakers? The answer might be, "He knows the right people." OK, that's your cue to ask, "Who are these right people?" There may be much conjecture on why a man gets a job, but there will be truth too.

Keep your eyes and ears open. You can't go to sleep on the job or someone will nudge you awake. But most people are almost wholly oblivious of what goes on around them. What do you see? What do you hear? You see the boss come out to Pete's desk and talk to him. He does that to your desk too, you say. But he comes out to Pete more often. Why? Is he a buddy of Pete's? Or is Pete needing his help? A chance remark might tell you something. The other day, I heard an executive state in a speech that he was a CPA. The mention seemed to me an unrelated fact. I asked one of his associates,

"Why did he mention that he was a CPA?" The man told me, "All of the top executives of his company are CPAs and, while he is in a different line of work, he has to keep reminding them that he is one of them." I could have dismissed the remark because it had no relation to the subject of the speech. But I noted it, asked a question and got some information. This is how I suggest you keep your eyes and ears open. Make notes of what you see and hear. Then ask questions.

Check on management development

Many companies have management development plans that call for the collection of the records on all promotable employees. The object of such plans is to bring potential managers to the attention of management, to tell the kingmakers about good men. A company with a management development plan usually tells the new employee, "After you have been here for a period and have proven yourself, you'll be included in our management development program." Most of these plans call for:

Ratings of employees at regular intervals,

Counseling of employees at the same intervals.

The rating sheets call for all supervisors to study their men and rate them on work factors.

The counseling allows the boss to talk over the man's work with the man at intervals. It gives the employee the latest word on how he is doing.

How to check on your company's management development plan

If your company has such an activity, here are some checks to make.

1. *How does your boss handle the counseling interview?* This is the big weakness in most of these plans. No one has trained the boss to handle this interview. He says, "Look, Sam, I got this rating sheet on you and personnel is after me to get it in, but I got to run to a meeting in ten minutes." With that start you know how important the interview is to your boss. You want to talk about your work, and your problems, and he has to run to a meeting. Another boss may talk about his problems all through the interview. He is supposed to talk about your problems, offer some suggestions about your work. The instructions tell him how to do this, but he was too busy to read them, or he has forgotten.

2. *Does anybody get promoted?* Of course, a boss moves up and his assistant takes his place. But does a man ever move from another department to take such a job? And if so why? Is it because management development had rated him higher than the assistant who might have moved up? Didn't the assistant want the job, what? Try to check associates on this.

3. *Are the middle-management men for it?* In most companies there is much complaint about the way the management development plan is handled. The supervisors are called into a meeting to learn how to use the forms and how to handle the interviews. One executive told me, "The boss told me to take back the forms and not rate my men so high." He said top management would be asking us, "Why don't you promote these guys with all these good marks?" Another executive states, "Ours works well. It got me two promotions."

4. *What is management doing to train the managers?* Lack of training is the weakness of most management development plans. Most managers do not understand how to counsel with subordinates. One man told me, "My boss called me in for this interview and talked the whole time about the trouble he was having with the transmission in his car. He mentioned my work a couple of times, but always we'd get back to that transmission." Other managers do an excellent job, handling the interviews well.

5. *Who is included?* Usually this is determined by the type of job or the salary rating. Your boss can tell you this. You might be eligible and have been overlooked.

6. *How do you get on?* If your company has a management development plan you want on it. You want your records and ratings where the kingmakers can see them. I'd suggest you get on, no matter how the plan is run in your company. It is better to be an in than an out.

The kingmakers know about management development

They put out the money to buy all of the forms, they approve setting up the procedures, the production of the training materials. They are so often too far away from it to know whether or not it is working well. But they know that the data on the forms tell them what the company has in the way of promotive manpower. And when a job is open, what is easier than to send for the folder of forms on one, two, or more men? The plan brings to the kingmakers' attention men they might not have known well. And in doing this it gives the men a break.

There is one other plus to most of these plans. Your rating is not made finally by your boss alone. Most plans call for a review of the rating your boss gives you by your boss' boss. They sit down and discuss you, and what your boss thinks about you. This brings you to the attention of your boss' boss. If your boss is enthused about the work you are doing, his boss knows it.

Management development helps you

If your company has a management development plan and you are on it and have something to recommend you, you are on the way up. That's why it pays to investigate what your company has. Your boss may not think much of it, but it does serve as a manpower inventory, no matter how it is administered. I suggest, "Get your name in the pot."

Check training plans

Perhaps your company does not have a management development plan. But it may have training plans from which you can benefit. Some companies have both. The first question to ask about any training plan is, "How can I get on it?" Ask your boss or the personnel department manager about any such plans. If you are fingered as a management trainee, you have attracted somebody's notice. That somebody represents the kingmakers and, if you handle yourself right, you are on the way up.

How about management clubs?

A factory supervisor told me that he was attending a meeting of his company's management club. "Who is eligible for this club?" I asked. "Everybody in management from my level up," he explained. In his shop there was the top man. Under him were four executives at the second level, then twenty-two men at the next level. The supervisor was at the lower level. "What do you get out of this club?" I asked. "We listen to talks on management," he answered, "but the big thing I get out of it is that contact with the other managers. The big boss attends every session and you usually get a chance to have a few words with him." In some towns these management clubs include the supervisors from most of the local businesses. The kingmakers look upon such clubs as a training activity. If there is such a club in your community, get into it. It puts you where the kingmakers can notice you.

Check personnel policies

I heard a personnel man make a speech in which he stressed the great manpower waste by the common mandatory retirement at age sixty-five. His company didn't retire men at sixty-five. I asked, "Holding on to these old fellows keeps the younger men from advancing, doesn't it?"

"Some," he admitted. "But we can't afford to lose that experience."

If your company retires men at sixty-five, a man who has just a few years to go may be turning over his power to those below him. This could affect your promotions. Ask yourself, "Is this man going to be the power when I come up for promotions?" Check any personnel policy that could affect you. It is well to know the personnel department and understand what part it has in promotions.

Look out for you

I worked for a company that sent some of its promising young men to the Harvard Business School. One day a young man approached me and told me that he would like to get on this program. I asked about his education and found that he had not completed college. I brought this up as a reason why he might not be eligible. "But they have included some fellows who have not completed college," he said. He had done some checking before he approached me. This is what I suggest you do. Be alert to such opportunities, management development, training, management clubs. Check them out. If you feel that the activity will help you advance, ask to be included. You can't lose, and you may be taken in.

How to impress the kingmakers

In national politics, the kingmakers are the people, the local political bosses, the workers in the wards. The local political candidate gets a group together and has them go out and ring doorbells. Those doorbell ringers are kingmakers. The man for whom they are ringing doorbells must have done something to impress them.

In company politics you have to do most of your own doorbell ringing. But the process is much the same. If you want to go up in the company, you have to get your name and your work before the ones who can vote for you.

Get the kingmakers' favorable attention

The key word in this heading is "favorable."

The other day I saw a young man at the country club with a growth of shaggy whiskers. I asked another young man who he was. The second man told me and I asked, "Is he celebrating a centennial or something?" He answered, "No, he's just beatniking it around with a couple of other guys with whiskers."

The young man with the whiskers made the first move open to young men in business. He attracted attention, but unfavorably. You want favorable attention. A young man said, "How can I get the man's attention? I have no business to transact with him, no contacts at all." Well, you are around the place, aren't you? And he's around the place. OK, get the kingmaker's attention with these four simple tools—appearance, movement, dress, voice.

Appearance. Your looks are what they are, but you can do some things with them. Look like the kind of man the power wants to promote.

Movement. As you move, you're tall or short, fat or slim, but when he looks at you what impression does the kingmaker get? Do you give the impression of a man on his way to get something done?

Dress. Do you have the correct clothes for the job you hold? Take a tip from the executives on this. They will feel that a young man who dresses like they do is about their kind of man.

Voice. When you speak to the kingmaker, does your voice help? If you speak slowly and distinctly and loud enough for him to hear and understand, you make one impression. If your voice is weak and you rush to tell your story and mumble your words, you make another. In Chapter 11 there are a number of suggestions for improving your voice.

Simple but effective

You may think these are simple things on which to judge a potential executive, but the kingmaker meets you and he hears you and he passes judgment. He can't help it. Note that not one of these factors, except perhaps your voice, have a thing to do with your work. If you had the opportunity to consider one of two candidates for promotion, which would you choose, the one that looked alive and alert, or the one that looked tired and sloppy?

If you had an appointment to talk to the top kingmaker in his office upstairs, you would try to make the best appearance possible, wouldn't you? Your Sunday suit, best shirt, newest necktie? OK, the kingmakers' assistants are observing you, everyday. Keep that in mind. Look and act and work so that those up above will approve.

This is the first step in moving up—attract the kingmakers' attention. You are in the position of the fellow hired to train the mule. As the owner watched the trainer hit the animal between the eyes with a two by four, the owner asked, "Why did you do that?" "Well, first you got to get his attention." Figure that as your first step, get favorable attention.

Politics takes many forms

Last year I worked with a company on some marketing problems. I was impressed by one young man, just thirty, who seemed to hold down a rather large job for a man that age. I asked one of the other men, "How does this young man come to be the manager of this department? Is he a relative?"

"No, but look at him," the executive said.

I had looked. The fellow rated tops on appearance.

"Have you talked to him?" the man asked.

When I nodded, he went on, "Does he give you the impression that he knows the score?"

I agreed and asked, "What else has he got?"

"Well, he is a mighty fine politician," the man said.

"What do you mean by politician?" I asked. "Just what does he do?"

Here is the answer pretty much as I got it. He came to the company out of college, he had been in the army before he finished school. He has done a good job on every assignment. He worked hard on every job. One boss had moved him up three levels by taking him with him when he had been promoted. When the boss had gone on to run another division of the company, he had recommended the young man for the boss's job.

Analyze that record and you find that

The man was willing to work,

He did well on every assignment,

He had made himself so valuable to his boss that the boss had taken him with him.

That sounds like the familiar success story. But I wanted to know about the politics.

"But what else has he done?" I asked.

"Well, he is into everything," the man told me. "You name it and he's in. The softball team, the bowling league, the country club, the public speaking club, the investment club. Walk through the office or factory with him and everybody knows him and likes the guy. Everybody is happy at his success."

What do you have in common with the power?

When you check the power in your company, you may feel that you have little in common with it. But check all the angles. What have you in common with any part of it? Perhaps it is a family or school tie, church, club, professional society, fraternity, hobby, golf, bridge, poker, tennis, the horses, boating, gardening. Don't laugh. All of these have been used. And others even further out. I talked to a young man on a training course who was assigned to a job in the factory. "Is there any politics on your job?" I asked.

"Yeah, you better chew Mail Pouch."

"Does your boss chew Mail Pouch?" I asked.

"Sure does, but he never buys it. He's always bumming it off of you."

You may say, "I don't like this kind of politics." Perhaps the boss doesn't either. But he might like a fellow who could help him teach a Sunday school class, or wield a second brush when he is painting his boat next spring. If you have any such tie, figure out how you can use it.

Use the direct approach

The most important power in your company as of today is your immediate boss. Start with him, his assistants, and any others in the department that you might feel will be up for promotion ahead of you. Impress these people, first by your work, your willingness to help out, your attitude and loyalty to the boss and the company. Talk to these people, ask them questions, listen to them. Make friends with them, play with them, show that you are a regular guy, that you deserve to be accepted as one of them.

I once was a department manager of a company and one of our number was selected to succeed our boss. The boss called us together to tell us about the appointment. As soon as the announcement was made, one of our group said, "I am sure that all of us will give your successor the same kind of cooperation we gave you." The man who made this speech was a likely candidate for that job. I'm sure that he was disappointed that he did not get it. But here he was on his feet telling management which side he was on. Politics, you say?

Yeah, maybe, but one of the first rules is to be on the side of your boss. Less than five years later the man who made the nice speech was made a vice-president of the company.

At one time I had a group of young men trained to take visitors on a factory tour. One day the factory manager telephoned me, "The president wants to go through the factory today. Your boys don't need to mind, I'll take him through." The man had an opportunity for an hour's contact with the power and he wanted to take advantage of it himself. I talked to a young man who had the job of driving the big boss up to the airport one day each week. "Gives me a contact with Mr. Big that I'd never get," he said. "Even though we talk baseball, he gets an idea of the kind of guy I am."

Any such contact with the power helps. When you get it, make the most of it.

Watch your step

Searching out the kingmakers is a political activity that you had better not talk about. A person who heard that you were doing this might think that you were doing it to take an unfair advantage of the kingmaker. But your desire is to know who is the power, so that you don't waste too much time trying to sell yourself to those who have no say. There is nothing crooked or underhanded about what you are doing, but it might be thought so by others who never thought of it. So get as much information as you can without outlining your objectives. And when you get it, use it.

Here are some thoughts on finding and working with the power in your company.

1. Know what you are looking for, the real power, not what seems to be the power.

2. Start with the power in your department. Find out where it is before you look above.

3. When you have your department cased, then go on to a study of the power above.

4. Check the plans the company has to help you advance:

Management development

Management training

Management clubs

Special courses

5. Attract the kingmakers' attention. First, by the job you are doing on your present assignment, then by the way you operate.

6. Work with the kingmakers. Use the ins you have with them to advance the cause of old Number One.

Now let's consider the most important kingmaker you have at this time—your boss.

9

Let's Take the Boss Apart

Your boss is your kingmaker.
You need him with you to move up.
You can't start moving up without his recommendation.
So let's examine this most important man.
Here are some questions:
  What is his age?
  Is he ambitious?
  What's his image?
  How about his health?
  What's his job record?
  Is he a good worker?
  What can you learn from him?
  What is his attitude?
  Who sponsors him?
  How does he rate socially?

What are his opinions?
How does he treat his help?
Is he honest?
How does he feel toward you?

The answers and you

The answers to each of these questions can tell you something about how your boss affects your desire to move up in your company. As you try to answer each, ask yourself, "What does this mean to me?" Here are the questions in more detail.

How about age?

If he is in his forties, he might have time for two or more promotions. That means his present job may have to be filled. It means men move up all along the line. If he is close to retirement, you can tell exactly when this move will come.

Then too, what is the age policy in your company? One executive said, "Our company has gone nuts on youth. We're moving out most of the old managers, promoting them out of the way." Another said, "In our company we let them go on as long as they can." Either policy affects the likelihood of your boss moving up. He may be one of the youth picked, or he may have to wait until one of the aged topples over.

Is he ambitious?

If he wants to move up in the company, he is not going to sit on this job and keep others from moving up. If he is moved to another department or division, he might take some of his people with him. That means more openings. One executive told me, "This executive has moved three times and each time he has taken his assistant with him." Think of the openings this has made in each of those changes. If your boss wants to move up, he won't refuse what the power offers him. He may not take you with him, but he makes a better job available to you when he moves.

What's his image?

If your boss looks like a potential top executive to you, he gives that impression to others too, others who might do something about it. Do they say he is a big fat slob, a bag of wind, or what? Do they rate him as a good operator, competent, a profit maker, a cost cutter? Do you think he is promotable, or has gone about as far as he can go? Since you are closer to him, you may perhaps not be impressed with his glamour that attracts outsiders. How much of this image is put on? The image your boss broadcasts is important to you because it helps him get the job ahead. If he broadcasts an image of capability, he is more likely to move up and open a higher spot for you. If he doesn't, you may have to move around him.

How about his health?

If his health seems good, there is little reason why he should not be assigned to the tougher job up above. But, if he has been sickly, he might be content to stay where he is. Then too management may be planning to move him on to another job so that his job may be given to one more vigorous. One president explained such a change by saying, "If we had left Mike on that job, he would have killed himself in a year." If your boss feels that because of his health he is as high as he can go, you have to look for channels of advancement that move you around him. You can get quite a bit of information about his health by observation. Does he look tired? Does he give the impression that he has hardly enough energy to live out the hour? Does he take pills before each conference in his office? How much time is he off on vacation? One executive told me, "My boss has been enjoying poor health for years, and the power above has been holding me as his assistant, for fear they'll have to replace him." This had been going on for six years, and the man questioned, "Will I live out my business life backing up this fellow?"

What's his job record?

You know that, if your boss gets the reputation of a producer on this job, he might be moved to another job that needs a producer. When a department's record is good, others explain it, "They got a lot of good men down there." This helps you because you are one of those good men. Let's say you were the manager of another department and needed a man. Where would you look for him? In a department that was making a record, wouldn't you? When you are being considered for promotion, the kingmakers may say, "He's been down there with Walter for two years and he must have learned something." Thus the good record of your boss benefits you.

If the department is slipping, it may be that a change is in the offing. Here the boss may not be to blame. But like the manager of the baseball team, he has to take the rap for failure. Of course, if his successor is picked from the department, this may mean a move up for you. Then too management may decide that his failure is due to the type of help he has and shake that up some.

You may feel that the record of your department is the

business of the boss. But it is your business too. If you **are** with a winner, you have a better chance of being selected.

Is he a good worker?

Is he willing to work? Does he take on some of the tough jobs himself or delegate all of them? Does he sit in the office while the department runs itself, or does he have some part in the running? How many afternoons each week does he take off to play golf? Who covers for him while he thus regains his health? How long does he take for lunch? Are his luncheon buddies of any help to him on the job? Where is he outstanding? How is he on detail? Does he want to do it all himself? Does everything have to be done his way? How much overtime does he put in? How much work does he take home? Have executives who fit the work pattern of your boss gone up in the company? As you ask these questions, you'll think of others. Answer them too.

What can you learn from him?

An executive complained to me, "Ed, as soon as I get a man trained, they take him away from me." I asked the head of the personnel department about this and he admitted, "He's the best trainer we got. We have boys he's trained in every department of the company?"

One young man gave me a whole list of complaints against his boss. I asked, "If this guy is so tough, why don't you quit or ask for a transfer?"

"I would, but I am learning so much that I can take this beating."

I've found that men will work for a martinet if they feel

they are learning something that will improve their ability to make a living. Ask yourself, "What have I learned from this man?" Check on some of the simple things that a boss should be able to teach you: saving time, observation, giving orders, handling help, buttoning up. Have men he has trained moved up in the company? A good trainer can teach you skills that will help you move up.

What is his attitude?

Yesterday I heard a man say, "My boss knows it all. If he was ever wrong, it was before I knew him." Does your boss fall into this class, or does he listen to suggestions? Does he tell you, "It might work, but why should we stick out our necks?" Does he check to see what the boss wants before he makes a suggestion? Is he always trying to change, or is he wedded to the *status quo?* Is he enthusiastic about the company, its business, its policies? Is he a complainer, a worrier? Your boss can't help showing his attitude to those around him, those above and those below. And is this helping him with the power above? Let's assume you had his job, which of his attitudes do you think are right for his job in your company at this time? And which of his attitudes are helping you? Then ask this most important question, "Is any of his attitude rubbing off on me?"

How does he rate socially?

This may or may not be important. In the large city it is not so much, in the small town more so.

One executive told me, "My wife plays bridge with the president's wife twice each week." He was telling me he had an in, wasn't he? Maybe the wife created it, but it meant that he was in on parties with his boss. This kind of social tie gets the extra contact the climber wants. If you are in a small town and your boss seems to be accepted by the right people, that may be a plus for him. If he has no social contacts, you know that he is not trying to use this type of politics to get ahead. Then is he the kind that the power would want to have around socially? Who are his golf companions? What couples does he go to the country club dances with? Check to see what social group he runs with and ask, "Does this help him in the company?"

What are his opinions?

What is he against? We define ourselves by what we are against. Just how important are the things he is against? I found a candidate for a job at the request of an executive and he told me, "I don't like this guy. He looks like an Englishman." This makes sense, doesn't it? Last week I read an article that reported a giant in industry did not like fat men. He wouldn't have a fat man working for him, and he did not like to do business with fat men. One boss told me that he wouldn't promote a man because the man wouldn't take a drink. These reasons sound silly when you see them in print, but you find that men in big jobs have them. A young executive told me, "My boss is a bird brain."

"Why do you say that?" I asked.

"He's always coming up with clichés like, 'Show me a man who holds his head high and I'll show you a doer.' "

The opinions mentioned here are all a bit on the bird-brain category. Your boss has good opinions too. Do these outweigh the screwy ones?

How does he treat his help?

The relations of your boss with his help and with others around the plant are important to you. If he is an SOB, the others say, "You must not have much backbone to take the guff that guy hands out." If he can be pushed around, they may feel you are a softie too. How do you rate your boss?

"He's a hermit," one man reports. "He goes into his office and closes the door. If you want to see him, he acts as if you are intruding." Another says, "If that guy says, 'Good morning, Hughes,' to me once more I'm going to pop him right in the nose." Another says, "The boss runs a tight ship. We work as a team. We all feel we are a part of it." You get both kinds of bosses, some good, some bad. Does he make fun of your suggestions, criticize before others? It is by little things that the worker judges the boss and the higher-ups too. Does yours say, "please," when he asks you to do things? Does he thank you when they are done? Does he send you to buy a pack of cigarettes from the machine? How does he handle instructions, complaints, compliments? Which of his practices would you change if you were given his job? Don't be discouraged if your boss doesn't rate high on these questions. Management experts tell us that most managers fail in their human relations tests.

Who sponsors him?

Who helped him get this job? Who keeps him there? What connections does he have with the men who decide who will be promoted. What does top management think of him? Is he somebody's white-haired boy? Is he a success or is he just filling a spot on the chart? What do you gain with those above by being known as one of Henry's boys? Then what man or men is he sponsoring? Does he have a group of assistants that he is trying to move ahead? Are you a member of this group?

Is he honest?

Does he level with you? Does he tell the truth? Is he a credit grabber, reluctant to share credit when he should? Will he tell you he is trying to boost you and then do what he can to scuttle you behind your back? How does he treat the men who are ambitious to get his job? Does he play favorites, and insist that he doesn't? Does he take the blame for department mistakes or try to find a goat?

His feelings toward you

If your company has a counseling program, you get an idea of how the boss feels about you at the time of the counseling. He rates you good or fair or poor, and tells you why. Perhaps he tells you that he feels you have promise but that you have to improve in certain ways. He may suggest some study or training you need to help you do your job better. I asked a young man how he was doing on a new job. "The boss brings me into all of the meetings," he said, "even asks my opinion at times." You know from this that the boss feels that this young man has promise. What indications have you that show how your boss feels about you? One man told me, "I doubt if he knows I'm there." If you feel that way, figure out how you can change that picture. You're there and you want to be noticed. If personnel suggested you for another job, what would your boss say? Would it be, "Yes, he's ready," or "I don't think he is quite ready yet?" Or, "OK, take him, he's not helping me too much?" If your boss feels you are a comer, your job is to prove it. If he doesn't like you, tells you so or rides you continually, ask him why. He is the kingmaker as far as you are concerned. You need his recommendation to go up.

What does this analysis make you?

One executive who read this chapter in its original form said, "Ed, a fellow who asks these questions about his boss makes himself out a cool, calculating operator, doesn't he?" He does that, and I admitted it. Then I asked, "You know any young executive who has done it?" He admitted he hadn't. Perhaps you haven't either, but a lot of men have asked these or similar questions, perhaps not all, but some of them. They have done it on the theory that, if you plan to do or die for old Uncle Boss, it might pay to see what he can do for you in return. I admit I didn't do this when I was moving up in company organizations, but last week I went back and made these checks on seven of the bosses I had in the past. Here is what I came up with:

The scores of seven bosses. Going back over a career in business, I have selected seven of my past bosses, seven that might be called kingmakers, and have rated them. Here is what I show:

Ambition: All rated over 90 per cent on this factor.

Five of the bosses were from ten to fifteen years older than I was. Two were younger.

On personality, the average was high. They looked capable and were.

On ability to handle their jobs, I rated each man good or excellent.

On health, six were in good health, one dragged.

On training of men, four did no training, two were good at it, one made passes.

On attitude, four were optimists, one was a fence straddler, and two were cautious.

On human relations, two were excellent, three were good, one was average, one was poor.

As a politician, two rated 80 per cent, the others 90 to 100.

On sponsorship—every one of the seven was promoted to better jobs. One went up to chairman of the board of a company, one to be a president, two to be vice-presidents, and the others to higher executive jobs, with perhaps five or ten years to go.

All of them worked.

Five of them knew enough to keep their mouths shut. Two sounded off at any time on anything.

All were acceptable socially.

Six were honest, one was tricky.

All had good company attitudes.

All seven recommended me for promotion.

How a boss can harm you

I asked a personnel manager, "What are the reasons middle-management men give when they ask for transfers?" Here are some of the reasons he gave:

The boss keeps you under cover from the higher-ups.

Says you're not ready when a promotion is available.

Has a negative attitude, is against everything.

Doesn't back you up, runs out on you.

Can lie to you with a straight face.

Grabs credit for your good work.

Is so aggressive for himself that the other managers don't trust him or any of his help.

Will sacrifice you to help himself anytime.

Is inept as a manager.

Is an outcast socially.

Owes everybody money.

Borrows money from his men.

Doesn't like you or is prejudiced against you.

Is out of step politically.

You easily see why any of these qualities in your boss can be harmful to you. If your boss has one or more of them, figure out how much these deficiencies can hold you back. But again don't kid yourself. A new boss you transfer to may have some of the faults too. Do what you can to check that before asking to be sent off over the hill.

Strive for the ideal relationship with your boss

In a letter he wrote, one personnel manager gave the bit of advice I have used as this heading. He explained, "The young executive should so operate that the boss labels him, 'my man,' so that the boss is proud to tell others, 'Bruno's my boy, I trained him, he works hard, he learns fast, he is willing.'" Such a boss will recommend the man for any job he can fill, and will protect him from promotion to a job the man can't handle, even though the man may want the job.

This is an objective to set for yourself. Get your boss to boast to the power above, "Chuck's my man, I trained him." When he does this, he is taking credit for your development and experience and shows that he will continue to take credit for you as you climb the ladder.

When to consider asking for a transfer

This critical examination of your boss may show you that you work for a man who can help you advance, or for one under whom your chances to advance are poor. If you find the former, you work for that label, "The boss's man." If your analysis indicates any of the following, you might want to get out or ask for a transfer.

The boss has too many of his own clique to take care of and so competition is too tough.

He is out of favor with the powers that be and has been passed over on a number of promotions.

He doesn't want to go up and leave his job open to you.

He has faults that may work against your promotion.

You don't like him and are not learning anything from him.

He doesn't like you and shows it, even tells you he doesn't like you, your work, or anything about you.

Don't rely on your opinion

You may feel that you are justified in asking for a transfer on any of these reasons or others not mentioned. But don't rely on your judgment. Ask others about your analysis. Cite cases and examples. Ask men in the company and men outside. Before you ask your boss for a transfer, have your reasons lined up and written out. Lots of men want transfers. Some have justification, others want only a change. Some you ask may feel your reasons are insignificant, some will assume you don't have what it takes to stand up to the job. State your case and listen to what they say. Don't try to justify your opinions.

If you try to argue, they will assume, "This guy didn't want any advice anyway." But don't ask for a transfer without a careful study of what this means. Think the move through, before you start action.

Know your boss and how he can help you

Your boss may be a good guy or a tough one to work for. But that's not what you want to know. You want to know how he can help you advance. So know him, learn all you can about him. Then estimate what that knowledge means to your advancement. Here is your plan:

1. Examine your boss critically in terms of how he can help or hinder in your drive for promotion.

2. If you feel he can help, work to get his label stamped on you. You want to be one he calls, "My boy."

3. If you feel he can't help, try to figure out what you can do to get out from under him and under a boss who can help you move up faster.

If your plan calls for getting the boss to label you as his man, there follow some suggestions that will help in that activity.

10

Play Smart Politics with Your Boss

You want him to call you, "My boy."

OK, why not work purposely to attain that status with him?

He is the first man you want on your side. Others above later, but he is the most important right now. So play smart politics with him.

Some executives are good at this, others not so hot. What's the difference? The other day I was in the office of a top executive when he got a long distance call. I asked if I should move into his secretary's office. He nodded. I moved and started a conversation with the young lady about working politically with the boss. "Advice on that could help so many men," she said. "Some of the men who come in here rub the boss the wrong way."

"And others?" I asked.

"They sail through. Why is that? Nice fellows too. I like them but somehow they get under his skin."

"You think it may be because they don't know how to work with the boss?"

"Maybe so, but how long should it take them to learn?"

Not long ago I was talking to the president of a company about a course in management practices he felt his supervisors needed. When we had agreed on the details, he turned me over to an assistant with these words, "Fred here will handle all the details of this. You'll deal directly with him. He is general manager of the division and, Ed, he's my strong right arm."

My strong right arm. If your boss says that about you, you are in. And I can assume that a lot of work has gone into your achieving that status. You might call much of that work politics.

In another company I work with I heard an executive tell his assistant, in a jocular way, "Remember, now, you're not indispensable." How did the assistant get on that basis with the boss? He did the things an assistant should do to win the confidence of the boss. The boss believed in him. They were working together politically. What does this type of association mean to you?

You both gain

If you work right politically with the boss, you both gain, but you gain the most. Think of these benefits——

You work closer to the throne.

You are in on things.

You are sent on important errands.

Your advice is asked.

Your suggestions are accepted.

You are given more important jobs.

You gain the respect of others.

Your job is more interesting.

You can probably think of other benefits. If so, make a note of them. Working right politically with your boss is the first step to any promotion.

Here are some suggestions on how to do that:

Be for him. A personnel manager told me, "Loyalty is an old-fashioned word." But politically loyalty is one of your best tools in working with your boss. Perhaps you know some man who seems to use every opportunity to stick a knife in the back of his boss. What do you think of such a fellow? Don't answer. I know. You wouldn't trust him far, would you? So be for this boss of yours.

Let others know that he is your candidate, your standard-bearer. Boost him, his record, the work of your department. Watch such remarks as, "My boss is OK, but. . . ." Cut out the buts. He's OK by you. Let everybody know that. Watch any remark that could reflect on him. If anyone else depreciates him, go to bat for him. You'd expect him to go to bat for you, wouldn't you? Determine his political objectives and try to help him achieve them. He is trying to impress Mr. B. OK, think of your idea in relation to its appeal to Mr. B. Give him your thoughts on how he can impress Mr. B. Think too in terms of his competition. One of the other department managers has just come up with an idea that has top management's attention. Can you think of something that might bring similar attention to your department? Tell the boss that you are for him but go a bit further, show by your suggestions that you mean what you say.

Find out what he wants. What is his ambition? To stay on the job he holds, or to move on to another job? He says, "I want to hold this job until I retire." Is this really true or is it face-saving because he has been passed up for promotion? If you know what he wants, maybe you can help him attain his goals. A boss I had came into my office one day and asked, "What do you think of this idea?" He then described a plan he had hatched up to take over another department and completely reorganize it. I thought the plan was good. The department in question needed the reorganization. "How can I help?" I asked. He wondered if I would help him lay out a presentation to the powers to sell them the idea. I laid out the presentation and he sold the idea, but I never could have helped if I didn't know what he wanted. Thus I made some capital for me because I knew. You say, "My boss never talks about his ambitions." Well, ask him. If that doesn't work, ask him about yours, get his ideas and opinions. If he'll talk about you, in time he will talk about himself. Know your boss's wants and desires and you may be able to help him attain them.

Help him to be right. We all want to be right and it is not good politics to tell the boss that he is wrong. You do better if you agree, oppose and you may start a fight. But there are times when you can't wholly agree. Perhaps he wants to make a move that you think is wrong and will be harmful to the department. Don't take the attitude that it's no skin off your shins. You're with him, remember. You want him to be right always. Do these two things: agree on the unimportant phases of his plan; ask questions about the important, the ones you feel will bring harm to the department. You might give him a list of reasons against the move. Let him read these, study them, and decide. Make up a sheet that gave both the "for" and "against" reasons. The two lists make your memo seem more objective and fairer too. Your excuse for doing this is that you want to be sure we have considered every angle. Note that "we." In any objection to a decision or policy, use this "we." It is not the boss alone, it is all of us.

One executive told me, "But my boss is one of these guys that is always right." This makes the disagreement tougher. But, if he is going to make a mistake that will affect him or his department, you want to do all you can to help him avoid it. You might ask him to study it awhile. This will give you time to dig up arguments against it. If you feel you must disagree, don't do it in front of others. This causes him to lose face. Do it in private. Then too don't argue because you think. Get the facts to back up your reasoning. Let's say that he tells you to do something that you feel is not right. You might try passive resistance. Stall until he puts on more pressure, and organize your reasons why this is not the thing to do. And remember this, his proposed decision may not be as bad as you think it is. But don't give up. Ask the questions, talk to others about it, make up the list of pros and cons. An executive should have all of the facts before he makes an important decision.

Not, "I told you so." If he insists on going through with the project that you opposed, move in and do all you can to make it a success. Then, when it flops as you predicted, don't be the first to say, "I told you so." Don't say that at all. He probably remembers your opposition. Supposing he doesn't remember it and says, "That scheme of yours wasn't so hot, was it?" What now? Admit that it wasn't so hot, don't tell him that you did not want to try the plan. Suggest your plan now and you'll no doubt get to put that into effect. "I told you so" may give you some satisfaction, but it is always lousy politics.

Work his way. You may be an independent who likes to do things your way. This is fine. Your independence indicates that you will do jobs without waiting to be told. But don't carry it too far. If the boss tells you to draw a line on the chart with red ink, don't do it with green ink because you like it better that way. Do it in red ink, his way. If he says, "Lay off" on a project you propose, "lay off." He may know something that you don't know. If he wants you to bring in problems and suggested solutions, don't bring in problems without the solutions. Be ready to say, "This is what I suggest we do about it." Then call things by his names. He calls a plan a project. OK, you use the word project too. If he wants you to leave the door of your office open, leave it open.

One man asks, "My boss is a credit grabber. If I do anything good, he'll take the credit for it." OK, do the job as well as you can anyway. Remember your advancement depends on the record he makes. You don't want him to claim credit for a poor job, do you? The wife of a friend, who complained that his boss always grabbed the credit, said, "Think how he feels. He hasn't the ability to turn out the job you do. I feel sorrier for him than I do for you. You can do it, he can't." But don't you feel sorry, help him make a record. If he is open to ideas or suggestions, offer him ones he might like. One boss I had said, "Tell me the cost first, before you go into the other details." Many times I had a proposal that needed a buildup first. But he wanted the cost first and that's the way he got it. Present ideas in the way he wants them presented. Remember that your boss thinks the way he works is right. He feels that anyone who works his way is working right. You may think that it would be better to change some things around, but don't do it unless you get his approval. By working his way, you show yourself a politician who can get along with others.

Talk his interests. You do this when you talk about the unimportant things, baseball, golf, fishing, boating, the performance of his car. But he may feel about this small talk as a friend of mine, a purchasing agent. The friend tells about salesmen who come in and ask him about his family and his golf game and other personal stuff. "I blast them though," he says. "I tell them, 'You're here to sell me something, cut out the chatter and tell me what the hell it is.'" Try to switch conversation about the small and the unimportant to more important subjects. You know he is interested in such things as doing a good job for the department, keeping his boss off his back, making a record that will move him up in the hierarchy, cutting costs, increasing profits. When you bring in your pet project to the boss, forget your interest in the project and think of his. The interests may be identical, then they may not. Thus, think of what your project will do in connection with what he wants to do. Ask, "What do you think the powers up above will think of this?" Or, "Check these cost-cutting estimates and see if I am right." With this approach you are talking his interests, and he is more likely to listen. When you have an idea or plan to present, think of this question, "What does he get out of it?" Now shape your story to make what he gets the most important factor. Let's say you want to move a production line a few feet so that you can get the loaded trucks through easier. He'd go for making a better path for the trucks but supposing you would save man-hours? Would he be more interested in that? Present your plan but make sure that he sees what he gets.

In talking to the boss, you can take two courses:

One, tell him what he wants to hear, and

Two, tell him the truth.

But in either case, tell him what your idea means to him.

Tie your interests to him. You want to go up, he wants to go up. In this way you are two of a kind. Let him know that you want to go up, that you are ambitious, that you are willing to put out what it takes. A good manager needs contact with his subordinates—to get information, to get suggestions, to check on interest. Your boss knows this, he is glad to know that you are his kind, that you are with him, that you want to work with him on a "one for all and all for one" basis. The "we" idea that I have suggested earlier is a help in this. This is our department, our project, we are working together to make it a success. One man asked me, "Supposing he asks, 'What do you mean, "we"?' What then?" Seldom will that question be asked. If the boss is shooting for the job above, he wants all of the allies, all of the boosters he can get. And even if he can't see how you can help much right now, he knows you never can tell. He knows too that it is better to have you with him than against him. If you are with him, why shouldn't he be with you?

Take a sheet of paper and make a list of ways your interests and your boss's interests coincide. Then talk about these common interests to him.

Fight his battles. This may help you get your throat cut, but you are into his battles whether you want to be or not. Be prepared to defend his actions, policies he sets up. If you know that another manager is out to get him, help him watch that manager, offer suggestions as to how to counteract the bad guy's moves, bring him any information you may get. Ask his advice about your role, about whom you have to watch, what care to use when you are working with the villain's department. If he is feuding with another manager, ask him to tell you the background of the feud. He may advise, "You stay out of it." This would be a break for you. But, if he wants you in, stay in. Battling for the boss may get you in trouble. The bad guy may move up, your boss might be out of a job and you with him. But you have little choice. By holding the job you hold, you are in the fight. Perhaps you are one who likes this kind of fight but don't go in swinging. First, talk to the boss about your role. Play it as he wants you to.

Live with his weaknesses. Last week I called on the top executive of a firm. Three times during our visit he said, "We are not comparing apples with apples." I noted that his associate who was with us seemed embarrassed at this repetition. No doubt your boss has some of these failings, the use of clichés, the pontifical pronouncements, expressions such as, "to make a long story short." Of course, you didn't agree to take this boss for better or worse, but this is the boss, you can't change him so forget his minor faults and live with them. In spite of these faults, he is doing a good job, isn't he? Then let's say he is a man from another generation. He can't help but have the ideas of his generation. "Coffee breaks are for the birds." "Union leaders are all crooks." Don't spend any time trying to argue him out of these beliefs. One man told me, "He won't turn up his hearing aid. He wears it but he keeps it turned off. So I gotta shout." Remember this, the old resist change. The boss who was brought up in a world twenty years before yours can't possibly go along with some of the accepted ideas of today.

One assistant told me how he had stopped his boss from sending out inspirational letters to the employees. He told the old man what the mailings cost. "When he saw that they cost $38 each, he wasn't so anxious to send them out." The assistant explained, "I couldn't tell him that the letters made him appear a screwball. He thought they were works of art."

If some fetish of the boss bugs you, try to think up some devious way to get him to lay off. That's good politics. But don't criticize the activity or habit. Learn to live with it. Remember these failings make him a character. And maybe he wants to be a character.

Keep him informed. Your boss travels in one group, you travel in others. He hears some things from his group, you hear others from yours. He may not be interested in gossip, but, if you feel that he should know about anything you hear, pass it on. He would probably like to hear about rumors quickly before they get time to build up.

Bring him information that you feel he wants. But use discretion, collect the information, sort it, and give it to him. If you have any doubts about information you come by, ask him if he wants it. He has eyes and ears, of course, but help him with yours.

Protect his status. The other day I was visiting an executive. He said, "We'll have to move out of my office and into one of the conference rooms. They are putting a carpet on the floor." I picked up my exhibits and we moved out. "You must be getting important, getting a carpet," I joked as we walked down the hall.

"That's a funny thing," he explained. "One of my assistants got that carpet for me. He told the office manager that a manager of my importance should have a carpet, that other men at my level did, and so I get a carpet. The office manager probably thinks I sent the assistant to say, 'Hurry up and get that carpet in the boss's office.' "

The executive did not need the carpet. He didn't care whether or not he had it. But it was a status symbol and one of his men got it for him.

You may laugh at the importance of such things as the name on the office door, the venetian blinds on the windows, the special type executive desk, and other such status symbols. But in some companies they are important. I asked the executive, "What good do you think the carpet does you?" He answered "None, as far as turning out better work is concerned. But it does have an effect on my gang. They don't want to work for a fellow who won't insist on his rights."

I have seen many such instances where employees go to bat to arrange such status symbols for the boss. Maybe you'll never get such an opportunity. But if you do, move in and do your bit. It is good politics and the boss can't get mad at you for it, can he?

Check your performance. How am I doing? That's what you want to know. Are you meeting his expectations? Your boss should be able to let you know how you are doing, to tell you where you stand, to advise you in planning improvement. If your company has a rating plan, the methods of doing this are laid out for your boss. But, if your company has an organized rating procedure and your boss never uses it, why not stage a rating interview of your own?

How to stage a rating interview with your boss

The questions that follow give you an outline for such an interview. The first step is to explain to the boss what you

want to do. Then ask for a time when he is free from inter-
ruptions so that you can talk undisturbed by secretaries or
telephone messages. Ask for thirty minutes at least. Then start
your interview with this introduction.

Explanation. I need some help and I am sure you can give
it to me. I want to improve, to make myself ready for promotion, and so I would like to ask you some questions about
how I am doing, where I stand now and how I can improve.
It is difficult for me to answer these questions, but you have
watched me work and are in a better position to help me
analyze myself. I have some questions here to help you in
this analysis. And while I am not asking for applause, the
first of these questions is:

Where am I good? I suggest this question first for most
bosses will be glad to tell you where you are meeting expectations. After he has answered this one and has given you a
few pats on the back, ask

Where am I falling down? He has given you the good news,
so now he won't hesitate to tell you some of the bad. Don't
try to alibi on any of his opinions by "Well, the reason for
that is. . . ." Ask questions about the criticism. The next
question is

Where do I need improvement? You might get specific
about this and mention knowledge, skills, attitude, personal
habits. You might quiz him on each duty listed in your job
description. The next question is

What training do you suggest? Get his ideas on this together with his thoughts on how you can do it while on the
job. Another question to ask is

Have I the potential to move up in the company? He may
mention some changes that are in order. Ask questions about
these changes.

Caution. I have given you only five questions here, but these are basic. You can add others to cover special interests of yours. But remember this. The purpose of this interview is to help you. You want help in developing ways to improve any poor performance on your part. Even though the boss rates you high, tell yourself, "The boss thinks I'm doing fine, but I can do better, I know." Don't feel you have it made. Use the strong points he mentions to help you get better, ask his help on the shortcomings so that you can work nearer your full potential.

Hold his interest

Then when you embark on a training program, keep him informed on what you are doing. If he suggested that you read a certain book, let him know that you have the book and report on your progress with it. Ask him questions about what you read in the book, discuss ideas with him, tell him when you have used one of the ideas and report on what happened. Think how he will feel when he can report to a boss above him who mentioned your name, "He's coming along, studying economics now, a book I suggested. I'm keeping in touch with his progress, talking ideas over with him. He is a good prospect."

It pays your boss to be interested in you. It pays you to hold his interest. Use every opportunity to get him to talk about you and your work, about your ideas for self-improvement.

Check your standing

Do you feel you belong? Are you in on things? Are you accepted? Once a fellow worker asked me if I had any idea why he wasn't named on a committee that the boss formed to study how the department could cut costs. My answer was, "I believe it is because the boss is never sure of you, he doesn't know whether or not you are for or against him." I had the same feeling about this coworker. He was pretty much a loner. He did his work well, but there was no way of telling where he stood. If the boss has any doubts about you, you want to know about those doubts. If a man had the reputation of being against changes, then he might not be a good member of a committee formed to study cost cutting. The boss knows that to cut costs you have to make some changes, and he might feel that this againster would talk the others out of some good suggestions. If you are left off a committee or off the bowling team, or out of a party, ask why. Perhaps you don't like committee work, or bowling, or parties, but you do want to be in. So ask. If the boss explains, "We never thought of you, Ossie," that's not too good either. Again ask why. The fellow who plans to advance in the company wants to be in on things. If you are not in, don't sulk and comfort yourself with the thought, "They don't appreciate talent around here." Check why. Then do what you can to change the habits or impressions that leave you out.

Solicit his help

Ask him for suggestions, for advice, for help. You do that when you ask him where you need improvement. Let's say you are having trouble handling one of the men in a different department. Ask him for suggestions on how to do this. Don't be afraid to bring in the personal. The doctor tells you that your little boy needs an operation. Talk to him about this. If you're planning to buy a home, ask him about the neighborhood, the financing. He is perhaps older than you are and has had more experience than you have in these matters. He may be able to steer you away from mistakes that proved costly to him. Then too he knows your financial status. If you are proposing to buy a home that is quite elaborate, and are planning to finance it on a shoestring, he may point out some of the troubles ahead. He may offer advice that will cut some of your financing costs. You may say, "I don't want to bother him with troubles of mine." That's a fine idealistic attitude. But he is your boss. He wants high morale in his department. Thus he is ready and willing to help. Then too, we all like to help the other fellow. As the boss listens to your problems, he comes to form a better impression of you. He may feel that you are a good worker but, when you ask for advice, you prove yourself intelligent too. Look where you came for advice.

Change habits that scare him

You can scare your boss. Not by being too forward but by the way you handle yourself with others in the department and the workers in other departments. Let's say you are an arguer. You go over to department B and get in an argument with a man there about some information you want from him. He doesn't want to give you the information. You argue with him about it. He takes it up with his boss. His boss calls your boss. Now your arguing has given your boss a new problem that he should not have. Maybe you are right, and you win the argument and get the information in the end. But you have caused a disturbance and lost some friends. Another department puts you on its bad guy list. And it doesn't make them feel too well about your department either. Thus your tendency to argue has given you and your department a bad reputation.

When I was young I had quite an argument in a meeting with a vice-president who wanted to spend some advertising money on an industrial product in a newspaper. My argument was that this was not a product to be advertised in newspapers. Later my boss called me in to his office and told me, "You were right. The V.P. admits you were right but he (the vice-president) wants to run this advertising to get Old Crumley off his back. Old Crumley makes only industrial products, he's being charged for a part of this advertising and he's bellyaching because he gets no ads. And you argue against it in front of all the V.P.'s men. Hegarty, there's a time to argue and a time to go along."

I was right, but I was out of place and the boss directed me to see this vice-president and apologize to him. Before I went up to see the big man, I made four layouts for advertisements on Old Crumley's products. I suggested that we run them only in the newspaper in the town in which Old Crumley had his plant. The V.P. enthused about the idea. He said, "This way we get off the hook for a small amount, don't we?"

I admitted we did, and the V.P. said, "Well, let's forget the argument. You showed me how to get this old guy off me." We shook hands on that.

Your habit that scares your boss may not be arguing, but it may be your letters to customers, the way you talk to customers on the phone, your forwardness with top executives. And the strange thing is that you may not have the least idea that these things bother him. In fact, you may think you are good at them. So ask him. When you are in for a rating interview with him or are staging your own, ask him, "Do I do anything that scares you?" Most of the habits that scare the boss can be easily corrected.

Be available

One of the best ins with the boss is your willingness to work, the regular hours, overtime, Saturday, Sunday, evenings. Take on whatever he suggests. If it is too much detail, ask him to provide some help. "Give me one of those fellows out in billing for a week and we'll get it out." This is what the boss likes to hear. Not long ago I heard the head of the company say, "Dusty refused to make a service call on Saturday. He knows this is a day-and-night business. He's through as far as I am concerned." Dusty probably had some big things planned for that Saturday, but by refusing to make the call he surely gave his advancement chances a setback. One company head described an executive thus, "That guy is the most willing man we got. He'll come in anytime we need him." If that fellow has the qualifications necessary, he is on the way up.

Your tie-in up above

Let's assume that you have an Uncle Charlie who is a vice-president. This may be good or bad, and you have to handle the situation mighty carefully. Your boss may feel he is training Uncle Charlie's boy, then he may feel you are there to spy on him. Your boss knows that you see Uncle Charlie, that he has you over to his house to dinner, that he asks you questions. This tie-in up above has added one more problem to the ones your boss has in managing you. What should be his policy toward you, favor you so that he will gain pull with Uncle Charlie? Work to get you transferred or promoted so that Uncle Charlie will be out of his hair? Keep you under cover so that you will know as little as possible to tell Uncle Charlie? In each course, there is a certain amount of politics, some good common sense, and some danger to you. But, you, how can you handle this situation without causing friction? First, analyze Uncle Charlie's motive in getting you into this department. Is he trying to check on the department, using you as his FBI? Or is he just trying to help a relative get a job? If you feel that his motive is the latter, let your boss know that.

Second, remember that your first loyalty is to your boss. Why not have a frank talk with him and discuss the situation in terms of what he wants in the company? If Uncle Charlie asks about the department, what does the boss want you to say? If he asks about the boss, what does the boss want you to say? If Uncle Charlie gives any hints, bring them to the boss. Uncle Charlie gives you an in up above. Try to handle yourself so that it also gives the boss an in. Let the boss know that you are for him first.

Third, ask the boss for ideas as to how to handle your situation with other men in your department. They know about Uncle Charlie and may be a bit suspicious of you because of the connection. Cultivate the friendship of these men. Let them know that the connection may help you or work against you, you sometimes wonder which.

When a promotion is up

When you hear that a job is available, one you might be considered for, ask the boss about it. If it is in another department, he may know nothing about it, but he will surely offer to check. Tell him that you want to be considered, and would like to know more about the details.

In starting out after any job, it is well to figure the politics of promotion in your company. When the higher-ups are looking for a man for a job and consult your boss, you have to consider these possibilities:

He could recommend you highly.

He may not mention your name.

He may depreciate your ability to handle the job.

He may approve of your ability but say that you are not ready yet.

He may offer a choice, name another man that the people up above have not thought of.

He may be so weak in his endorsement of you that the higher-ups start looking elsewhere.

The boss may be honest in any of these courses, then he may be playing politics. For instance, if he recommends you highly, it may be because he can see some advantage to him in your transfer. It could be, he may want to get rid of you. If he doesn't mention your name, it may be because he doesn't want to lose you. If he depreciates your ability, it may be because he would like to see another get the job or wants to hold you. That name he offered as a choice might be a relative or a fellow that he has been trying to get out of his department for quite awhile. He may say you are not ready yet because he wants to keep you and not break up his team. He may be weak in his endorsement because he is afraid to stick out his neck, he wants to keep you, or has another in mind for the job.

Consider each of these motives when you go to talk to your boss. Let's say that the appointment is in your department and he tells you that he is recommending another. Ask him why. State your qualifications. It would be well to think these over and have them written on a card as you talk to him. Your listing of your qualifications may refresh his memory on points that were not considered. It may not get you a reconsideration, but he will give more thought to you next time. Also, your story may give him the feeling that he owes you something. This may result in a raise, an assistant, or other consideration.

When your boss is promoted

A good politician should be prepared to do the right thing when he hears that the boss is to be promoted up into the hierarchy. If he had heard this on the grapevine before the official announcement, he would probably follow this procedure.

Congratulate the boss. Tell him you are glad to see him move up, that you hope your work helped him. You are sorry to see him go in a way for he has been a good boss and you have learned a lot from him. Suggest that if he ever needs a good man to give you a ring.

Ask about his successor. He may tell you the name of your new boss or he may say that he is not free to do that yet. If you are in line for the job, ask what he thinks of your chances. If you don't consider yourself in line, tell him that you will work with the new man just as you have with him.

Ask if you were considered. If you are in line and are not going to get the job, ask if you were considered. If not, ask why. If you were considered, ask, "Was there anything particular that worked against me?" If he gives a reason like age, ask, "Was there anything more important?"

Repeat the congratulations. Close the interview on a repetition of your congratulation.

When you are passed over for promotion

This can be serious to your ambitions to move up in the company. You have some things to find out. Are you ever going to be considered for promotion? You want to know this surely, for it will suggest that you had better look around for a new job. If the choice between you and the fellow who got the promotion was so close that a flip of the coin may have decided it, you want to know. If the man who got the promotion has a bit more tenure than you or an experience in a department or the field that you don't have, passing you over may be no slap at you. But in any case:

Find out what is what. Ask questions that help determine if your name is still in the hopper, or if it has been taken out. Do the kingmakers feel that you are promotable, that you have the ability to hold a better job?

Don't take a gypping lying down. If you feel that you were better qualified than the man who got the job, ask what goes on here. State your case as powerfully as you can. You have this, you've done this, you've made this record, and you get this kind of pushing around. Again I suggest that you make an outline of your story and talk from the outline. Don't write any letters to your boss or to those above him. Just talk your case to your boss. Letters indicate that you are a sorehead. By talking your case, you show that you are honestly steamed up.

Do the best job you know how

If you are passed up, don't sulk. Give your job all you have. Such an attitude shows the higher-ups that you have what it takes. Surely, you got a kick in the teeth. But you get a lot of those as you go through life. I had one boss who was passed up four times for a promotion to vice-president when he deserved the boost more than any of the men who got them. But today that fellow is president of the company. Each reverse made him work harder. It is a good plan for you. The hard work helps you.

Build character out of your reverses

A young salesman gave me an idea on this. He had just been fired from his job. I asked, "What are your feelings toward the manager that let you go?"

"Just what I told him. I said, 'Boss, you have to run this territory. If you think you can run it better with another man, you should try to do that.' "

The young man thought he had been given a raw deal. But he handled it well, didn't he? He couldn't have helped himself by calling the manager names, or blaming the company or its policies. So he bowed out gracefully, building character as he went.

Be honest about it

There are two kinds of politicians in the popular conception, the honest Johns and the crooked ones. I suggest you follow the lead of honest John.

One man listened to me talk about one of these suggestions and said, "Ed, that sounds like trickery to me." Perhaps so. But my suggestion is, "Be honest about it." You are trying to advance your interests; you are trying to advance the interests of the boss. You are willing to state that under oath, aren't you? What's tricky about that? You are working for the good of the boss, the good of the department, the good of the company, right out in the open. You are not trying to be fast, sly, cunning. I suggest you approach each one of these suggestions with the question, "Can I be honest in doing this?" If you can be honest, try the suggestion.

Cuddle up a little closer

You've heard the song of that title and, as I review the suggestions given in this chapter, I smile at how close these suggestions follow that title. But that is what you are doing. You are building a closer relation with your boss. Note that each one lets him know that you are for him, and are trying hard to do the best you can for him. I showed this list to a budding executive and he said, "Nobody can do all of these things." He's right. But, if you do just a few of these things that you are not doing now, you are working a bit better politically, aren't you? One man said, "I couldn't bring myself to do some of those things." OK, how about those you can do?

Yesterday I talked to a woman friend who had been a secretary to six men at the V.P. and president level. I told her about this book and this chapter. She said, "I could work politically with all of my bosses but one. He had interests that had nothing to do with business. I quit that job." There may be times when you run into such a situation. But in the ordinary course of a business life such instances are not common. If you work politically with your boss, he is more likely to stamp you as "my man."

To get to that stage where he has belief in you, I suggest:
1. Tell him that you are for him.

2. Demonstrate the truth of this statement at every opportunity.

3. Play his political game, whatever it is. Have him clarify your assignments.

4. Get him to think of you as "one of my boys."

Then use communication to build yourself politically.

11

Communication Is Politics

That's what the candidate for office is trying to do—trying to tell you that he is the best man for the job. In business you can't go around telling people that you are the best, that you should have the promotion, but the way you communicate with others tells them that you are the man to vote for.

You have two types of communication on your job:

Communication up—to your boss and those above you, and

Communication down—to those below you on the ladder.

In both types you have two objectives:

First, to tell what you want to tell simply and understandably, and

Second, to tell it in such a way that the receiver thinks better of you.

That second covers the political aspect of business communication. If the listener understands, he gets a better impression of you. This is true, even in the simpler things.

Let's say you throw a quarter to one of your men and say, "Here, Rudy, go buy me a pack of cigarettes." This is communication down. Rudy catches the quarter, goes off on his errand and brings the pack of cigarettes back to you. You don't even look up from the letter you're reading as he lays the cigarettes on your desk. The act is finished and you've made an impression on Rudy, haven't you? He may say nothing but he thinks a lot.

While we are with Rudy and the cigarettes, let's assume that Rudy catches the quarter, throws it back at you and says, "Go buy your own blankety-blank cigarettes." This is communication up. Rudy has told you that you have made an impression on him. He has also told you something about him.

But let's go back to the first case. Let's assume that, when you threw the quarter to Rudy, you said, "Will you get me a pack of cigarettes, please?" Rudy goes after the cigarettes. He brings them back. You thank him, open the pack and offer him one. He says, "No thanks, boss, anytime."

In these examples you and Rudy have done both parts of the communication job. You instructed, he understood, you gave him an impression of you. As the boss, your instructions were clear. What you said and the way you said it made an impression on Rudy. What he said made an impression on you.

Use the spoken, the written, and the visual

Once the president of my company asked me, "How can we get these people up above to understand what we are trying to do? I've talked and talked and they listen, but they don't seem to understand. If we can't get through to them, they'll close us down sure." This was important. If we didn't communicate better, we'd both be out of jobs.

We were a small division of a large corporation. The president had been trying to explain our business to a group of executives of the corporation, men that had been brought up in an entirely different type of business. He was getting nowhere. We sold a consumer product, the listeners' experience had been in heavy machinery. It would mean little to the corporation to close out our small company. It was peanuts compared with other divisions of the corporation. After a discussion we decided to make a presentation that asked for money to operate the company for the next year. We did this with charts and we finished the presentation with a quiz that asked the executives of the corporation to answer some questions about the business of the division. We got the approval of the budget, and the answers to our questions showed that our presentation had given the executives a better understanding of our business.

I cite this instance to show the value of using all three devices of communication. The president had talked to the executives, he had given each of them written reports, but until we added the visual to the other forms of communication, we could not make these executives understand. Thus you have three communication skills to develop—the spoken, the written, and the visual. Let's discuss how your communication can give a picture of you. First, speaking——

DEVELOP YOUR SPEAKING SKILLS

Speak up

In my management workshops, I have a man stand up and tell the group his name and the name of his company. Then I ask a stranger to the speaker to tell the group the man's

name and the name of his company. In eight out of ten cases
the second man cannot do this. The speaker has not made
himself clear. I then drill the group on how they should say
their names, slowly, distinctly.

You get this in introductions. A friend introduces another
to you and you hear, "Mr. Wumph of the Wahoo Company."
You hear mister and company period. Moral—if you can't
say your name so that another understands it, will he understand anything else you say? Why have the power saying, "He
mumbles his words."

Check your voice

Your voice helps in the first impression you give others. If
you don't know how your voice affects others, why not rent
a tape recorder over the coming weekend and talk into it and
listen to what you say, how your voice sounds. You can speak
louder and slower. You can put that second "g" in a word
like *"going."* Unless you have trained your voice for speaking
you will find a number of such minor corrections you can
make. When you have checked, you will have a better idea
of the impression your speaking gives to others. You might
try this exercise I give my grandchildren. When they say,
"yeah" or any of the other forms for "yes," I ask them to say
"yes." I do the same with "you." Then with "get."

Reading aloud is good exercise in developing the voice.
If your children ask you to read to them, do it. Read the
stories aloud with feeling. If the story is about a naughty
little pig, let your voice get the impression of naughtiness into
your narration. You'll be amazed at how much life and feeling you can put into those vocal chords of yours. Read to
your wife for a few minutes every night. As you read, slow

up, try to pronounce each word correctly. Ham it up a bit if you want to, put feeling into it. Most of us are all so sloppy in our speech that we can stand some improvement. You don't want the power saying, "His voice gets on my nerves."

Train yourself to use simple language

The other day a young executive asked, "I am developing a vocabulary of management words. What do you think of that?" I thought it was for the birds. Management books are full of such words, but I am willing to bet most managers don't know what they mean. The young executive thought that a vocabulary of such words would make him appear to be management material. Maybe they would but you are trying to present a picture of you as you are. Here's some tips on how you can do that:

Use simple words. By using simple words, you don't have to change your language when you speak to the top men or to the fellow on the bottom of the ladder. If you make a habit of using big words, the ones around you may peg you as a stuffed shirt. And stuffed shirts don't do too well politically. Simple words picture you as a clear thinker.

Use your own words. You'll be able to pronounce your own words and they will sound natural coming from you. Some of those words the young man learned out of the business review might have made the boss men look over their spectacles at him. For instance, I never say that something is of prime importance. Prime is not one of my words. I can easily say, "It's mighty important." "Mighty" is one of my words. Your own words picture you as you are.

Watch the cliché. The reason you should avoid these tired expressions is that you don't want the listeners to get the idea that your mind works in clichés. You want them to think that you are alive, alert, up and coming. If you want to express the thought you feel the cliché does well, state the same thing in your own words. Don't say, "We can't build on sand." Say instead, "We can't build on nothing." Same idea, but the latter is yours. And it doesn't date you.

Be specific. Let's say you tell the boss, "It will be more economical to do this this way." What do you mean by economical? Will you save time, money, labor, electricity, what? Why not tell what. You say he knows. Fine, but don't assume he knows, tell him. The boss likes his information spelled out.

Watch the capital "I." Too much use of the personal pronoun gives the other fellow a bad impression of you. Watch the "I think . . . ," or "I know" or "I want," or "I'd do it this way." You know others who do this and what do you think of them? Change the way you say this to "Don't you agree?" or "Isn't this what we want?" or "Don't you think this way would work?" This technique works well with those above you or those below you. With those above you show that you are not a know-it-all. With those below you indicate you want their advice or suggestions.

Use correct English

Incorrect English can tear you down. Last week I interviewed a young man for a job. In our conversation he made a number of mistakes in English. I asked him, "Why don't you work to correct those mistakes you make in English?" He asked, "They know what I mean, don't they?" They do, and, if you make any mistakes in English, the mistakes put a minus sign on you. Check to see if you make any of these telltale mistakes:

Double negatives: "I ain't got none." Correct, "I don't have any."

Gone and went: "I should have went." Correct, "I should have gone."

Know and knew: "I knowed that." Correct, "I knew that."

Good and well: "This works good." Correct, "This works well."

The objective: This is a bit more difficult to correct than the ones mentioned above. It is so tough that often radio and TV announcers slip up on it. The most common is, "Between you and I." Correct, "Between you and me."

It is easy to correct these simple mistakes. And if you make any, start work on them now. They mark you, not as a comer, but as a fellow who is too lazy to educate himself. And the lazy birds don't move up.

Learn to speak to groups

Public speaking is probably one of your strongest tools in making an impression on those above and below you. If the boss has two men for promotion, men of equal ability, one a good speaker and one a poor speaker, he'll probably select the good speaker. This may not be fair, but it is simple to explain. The poor speaker doesn't convince the listener that he knows what he is talking about, he fumbles, stumbles, doesn't seem sure. When I was in charge of the trainees for one company, one of the first subjects we taught was public speaking. We knew that, if a department manager heard a trainee do a poor speech, he wanted nothing to do with him. If you have had no training in speaking, I suggest you get it. Take a speaking course, join a Toastmaster's Club. Do something that will put you on your feet regularly speaking to groups. Even though your job calls for no speaking to groups, the training is good, for it will help you express yourself better in small meetings or to employees or bosses.

Use your big mouth to help

Spoken communication can help you politically if you:

Speak up—pronounce words, enunciate clearly.

Develop your vocabulary with the idea of making yourself clear.

Correct any mistakes in English you now make, and

Learn to speak to groups.

What you say, and how you say it is a great political tool that tells others much about you.

WORK ON YOUR WRITING SKILLS

Study your letter-writing ability. Get out a few carbons of business letters you have written lately and do this. First, think of the one who received it, then ask yourself, "Did I make myself clear?" Second, check the letter for any outdated expressions such as, "Yours of the 5th inst. received...." Doesn't it sound more like you to write, "I got your letter, Charlie...." There are many good books on letter writing. If you feel you have need for improvement in this skill, get one of these books and study it to see where you can improve. Remember you have to write letters to the boss too. It helps if he says, "This fellow writes a good letter."

Learn to use other writing devices too

There are a number of other simple devices that give the power a picture of you, the way you think, the way you operate. Here are some helpful ideas:

Use the outline. Let's assume you want to talk to the boss about a project. You impress him if you come into his office with an outline of the points you plan to cover. Take a small file card and write your outline on that. If he asks for a write-up, give him that later.

The outline does two things for you. It makes sure you cover the points you wanted to cover, and it shows the boss that you have taken the time to prepare. Use the same idea when you are speaking to those under you.

Number the points. The points on your outline could be numbered. You want the boss to approve three things. Your outline then lists the three: first, this . . . ; second, this . . . ; third, this. . . . This numbering shows the other fellow that you have an orderly mind. It is impressive.

Propose step-by-step procedures. The boss asks, "How will you teach the men to use this new machine?" You say, "Here is a step-by-step procedure I worked out." Then you explain, "First, he does this . . . ; second, he does this . . . ; third, he does this. . . . What do you think of the procedure?" What can he think? Of course, he can suggest some changes, but he is helping you work out your procedure.

Show advantages and disadvantages. This works well whether you are for or against the proposal. Take a sheet of paper, draw a line down the center of the sheet. On the left of the line show the advantages, on the right side the disadvantages. In the discussion with the boss or the help, you show the sheet, ask if the other can suggest others, and then discuss the points. By showing both sides you give the impression that you are being fair, that you feel you should be thorough in your analysis of the proposal. And it also suggests to the others that you have an orderly mind.

Write something. You say that 62 per cent of your production are the blue. OK, write the 62 per cent for the other to see. I may remember the figure from hearing you say it, but I'll be more certain to remember it if you write it out and leave it there before me.

Use the summation. One executive explained how he used this device. "I sum up what the deal means to us on a small card. The card shows what it costs, how long it takes, what we get out of it." You can use this idea with your group. You want 10 per cent more production next week. You put the 10 per cent on the card, show what it means in units, what they get out of it.

Show orderly thinking. Each of these writing devices shows two things, that you know what you want, and that you think in an orderly fashion. Both those above and those below see this. And management is always on the lookout for orderly thinkers.

USE THE VISUAL

One great help in getting over any communication is the picture. Psychologists tell us that 87 per cent of our impressions come through our eyes. Why not use that fact? Good communicators use the visual.

Visualize the deal

You want the boss to buy a new machine for your department. You go into his office to talk about it. He asks, "What is this thing, what will it cost, why do we need it, where will we put it?" You knew beforehand that he would ask those questions. Show him the machine, a photograph or a circular on it, then a sketch that showed where you were going to put it, a sheet on which you had written the cost and figures on what you would save per month through its use. Now you have a visual that answers all of his questions. And wouldn't the boss better understand what you wanted, and wouldn't he have a better opinion of you?

What will I show?

In any contact with your boss or the employees below you, ask yourself this question, "What will I show them to help explain?" It is not difficult to find something to show to help you get over your ideas. Find it and show it.

LOOK WELL IN MEETINGS

There are two types of meetings that are a part of your daily work. Those you attend, and those you run yourself.

Follow this plan in meetings the boss calls

In the meetings that the boss calls in his office or the meeting room, follow these ideas:

1. Keep quiet unless your opinion is asked.
2. Listen courteously to everything that is said by anybody, big and little.
3. Close to the end of the meeting offer your ideas but be brief.

On individual meeting assignments

When the boss asks you to cover a subject in a meeting, cover the subject as well as you can. Get the information on it, prepare this in outline form. Think of how you can visualize the subject. Make up some charts, use a blackboard, but hit the listeners in the eyes with your message. Harpo Marx says, "I like to see what I read." Your audience does too.

Follow these ideas in the meetings you run

The other day an executive told me, "This man runs a good meeting." The meeting manager had impressed his boss. When you run a meeting with no fumbling and no stalling, you impress everybody. Here are some secrets of running good meetings:

1. *Set an objective.* Know what you want the meeting to do. Is it to inform, to stimulate, to teach? Get this firmly fixed in your mind and then aim your meeting at that objective. If you have no objective, forget the meeting.

2. *Prepare.* Know what you are going to say. If you have a speech to do, rehearse it. Make an outline of the points to be covered in your speech.

3. *Use visuals.* Again I make this point. Let the group see what you are talking about. Use a blackboard or easel pad, but show as well as blow.

4. *Get them in.* The listeners want to take part in your meetings. They understand better and learn more if you plan to let them in. Ask some questions to see if the group understands, ask for suggestions, ask for advice. Ask one man for his opinion, then another. Get the listeners in and the meeting picks up.

5. *Button up.* If the meeting was to inform, check to see if they understand. If it was to train, check to see if they can do the task. Assume nothing. Check.

Your meetings mark you

The politician gains or suffers by exposure. The more the public sees him, the stronger its impression of him becomes. He's good, or he's a no good. And they are positive. They saw him and watched him perform. You are in this position when you run your meetings. The listeners see you, they watch you perform. Run meetings well and you give yourself a good image. Goof off on them and you lose a lot of votes. I say this from experience. Fumble around at your meetings and the listeners think you don't have much of any other kind of ability. But learn to run good meetings and you will have acquired skill that will help you advance.

Note. If your job calls for taking part in or running meetings, my book, *How to Run Better Meetings,* McGraw-Hill Book Company, New York, 1957, will be most helpful to you.

LEARN TO LISTEN

This is one of your strongest tools in communication. One of my friends, a factory supervisor, asked one of the toolmakers why he went to the union steward with a complaint. "Why didn't you come to me?" he asked. "I could have straightened it out in no time."

"But the steward's got time to listen to me," the man explained.

"Maybe he came to me once when I was thinking about something else," the supervisor explained. "He didn't think I was listening and so he told himself, 'No sense talking to that guy.' Now the union steward has made a shop-wide grievance out of that little peeve."

In my management clinic I ask the supervisors, "What does your boss do that irritates you when you try to tell him something?" Here are a few of the answers:

Fumbles through papers on his desk

Looks up a telephone number

Searches for something in his desk drawers. Says, "I had it here a minute ago."

Breaks in with a question such as, "Did the Indians win that ball game last night?"

Borrows a match to light a cigarette

Calls out instructions to his secretary

Looks out the window

Manicures his fingernails

Keeps repeating, "Go on I'm listening."

You probably can add some of your own to this list. But, if you have any of these habits, try to get rid of them.

Three steps to listening

I have a simple formula for listening which goes:

First, hear what is said.

Second, let the other know you have heard, and

Third, show an interest.

Check yourself against this formula. When the wife or the children tell you something, do you follow these steps? Do you make them feel their message is important? There has been a lot of educational activity for executives on listening in the past few years. If you want to improve this skill, I suggest that you get and read a book, *Are You Listening?* by Ralph G. Nichols and Leonard A. Stevens, McGraw-Hill Book Company, New York, 1957. The book gives you a more elaborate formula for listening well. It also suggests exercises to help you improve your listening skills.

COMMUNICATION MAKES OR BREAKS YOU

I have worked with engineers who had the faculty of making the most intricate process understandable to the layman, others who knew what they were doing but could not convince listeners that they did. I've seen men advance faster than others because they had the ability to use the devices mentioned in this chapter to make themselves clear. Check the skills mentioned and start working now on the ones on which you need improvement. Here is a review of this advice.

1. Communication can be of help to you in two ways:
    a. To help others understand you, and
    b. To make an impression on others.

2. In business three types of communication are important to you—the spoken—the written—the visual.

3. Develop your speaking skills including the skill of speaking to groups.

4. Work on your writing skills, your letters and use the other written devices that help make your meaning clear.

5. Learn to visualize. In every contact try to figure out how you can show something that helps the other understand.

6. Study how best to handle your performance in the meetings of your boss, and the meetings you put on.

7. Study the art of listening. The other fellow is trying to tell you something. Forget that you are busy and try to find

out what he is trying to convey. Let him know that his information is important.

Then another part of this playing politics in business is getting everybody with you. "Everybody?" you ask. No, perhaps you can't get everybody, but you want to get everybody you can.

12

Get the Votes of All

Last week I made a call with a salesman in a large factory. The policeman at the entrance greeted him cordially. The elevator operator asked, "How you doing, Chuck?" The receptionist in the lobby on the executive floor seemed glad to see him. While we waited for the executive we came to see, I asked, "You think these friends, that cop, the elevator operator, or the receptionist help you get business from this company?"

"Probably not," he answered, "but there is no sense having anyone against you."

No sense having anyone against you.

That's a good slogan to carry with you in your drive to the top. Get even the smallest with you. The baseball manager said, "Good guys finish last." But that is not true. It can't hurt you a bit to be known as a good guy. And it can help you.

There are three elements that help you make a success of your job:

First, your desire to work on the job,

Second, your ability to handle the job, and

Third, your capacity for getting along and working with the people above and below you.

This chapter offers suggestions for getting along with and working with the people around you, those above and those below.

IMPRESS HEADS OF DEPARTMENTS

You'll probably handle your contacts with these men as well as you know. You understand how they can help you get ahead. They might hire you away from your present boss or suggest you for a better job. To make an impression on these men above you, use these suggestions in your contacts with them:

Be prepared

Don't go into the big man's office unprepared. You want him to approve something, to do something. OK, spell it out for him. Tell him what you want specifically in ABC fashion. Don't assume he knows. If it calls for some of his employees doing some work, offer to help on this. Tell him why and give him some reasons why what you want is important, how he gains or the company gains by what you ask. Make an outline of the points you want to cover as suggested in Chapter 10 so that he will see you are trying to save his time.

Don't overtalk. Boil down what you have to say into as few words as possible. You want these figures. This is why you want them. This is how you plan to use them. Do this with as little talk as you can. If you give him a memo to read, keep quiet while he reads. You may talk him into approving what you want, then talk yourself out of the approval.

Forget conversation makers. Show by your manner and organized presentation that you want to conserve his time. Don't tell him he is busy. He knows that. If you remind him how the few minutes he has given you has kept him from doing something else, he is certain to feel more antagonistic about your proposal. You don't have to ask him how his golf game is, or tell him that you saw him at church Sunday. If he brings up those extraneous matters, all right, but don't bring them up.

Make yourself clear. When you contact one of the big men, make yourself clear. You start this when you prepare and make an outline of what you want to cover and use the devices mentioned in Chapter 11—the visual, the numbers, the summation. If you have any doubts as to whether or not you are making yourself clear, ask, "Am I making myself clear?"

Ask for advice and suggestions. You came to this man to ask him to do something for you. When you have explained what you want, ask, "Do you think this is a good way to go about this?" He might offer you some advice that will help you accomplish what you set out to do. Ask also if he has any suggestions for improvement. By asking his opinions, you compliment him. You give him the idea that you are open to suggestions.

Handle resistance with questions. If the big man balks at approving what you want, don't argue. Ask why he objects. Listen while he explains. He may have a better way, then again he may be objecting because this is not his idea. Ask enough questions about his objections and he will see that they are not as important as they seem.

Bring him in. If your deal will speed up production on one machine 10 per cent, ask him how much he thinks the company could spend for a machine that would do that? You have your estimate to use, of course, but he will be more likely to go along on his estimate. If he says he doesn't know, ask him if he thinks your figure is close. His estimates of this sort seem more sensible to him, so use his figures. Don't try to sell him yours. The difference in the figures will seldom make much difference in the results you claim.

Call him "Mister." In any contact with an executive above show you were brought up right. Call him, "Mister." His nickname may be "Butch," and everybody around the place calls him "Butch," but don't you call him "Butch." Call him "Mister" until one day he asks you, "Where do you get that 'Mister' stuff?"

Use common courtesy. Thank him for seeing you. If you ask for something, use, "Please." When you leave his office, thank him for the time.

Ask for what you want. You called on the big man to ask for something. Don't bow out without asking. Don't have him ask, "What do you want me to do about this?" If he asks that question, tell him exactly what you want him to do.

BUILD CHARACTER WITH EXECUTIVES AT YOUR LEVEL

In all of your contacts with the men at your level follow the suggestions given for working with the top men. The top men can order you to do something, or they can get your boss to issue the order. These men at your level can't do that. They have to use persuasion and you have to use persuasion with them. You no doubt lunch with these men, go around with them socially, play golf with them, deal with them on friendly terms. And these contacts help determine how you handle them and how they handle you.

What do you have to offer them?

The suggestions given may give you the thought that you are using these men for your benefit. This is true. But here is another truth, they are using you too. Perhaps it is because you are enthusiastic about things, you have a drive that they'd like to copy, you listen to them and show interest in their ideas, you can be sure it is something. Try to analyze what this is, what you have that attracts them, and don't cut off the supply. For if you have nothing to offer them, they are not going to run with you. They'll shift to others that have something to offer. Remember Chalky, that fellow that was your pal some years ago? You don't see Chalky so much now, do you? Why? Is it because Chalky can't see how you can help him, or do you feel that he can't help you? Can you explain why? Think of this mutual interest in the suggestions that follow. You can't succeed as an "all for me" operator. You have to give as well as get. And remember this, the fellow that gives most, gets most.

Mix with them

Don't be a loner. Go to lunch with these fellows. Talk to them. Bowl with them, golf with them, play gin with them. Get into their football pool, match them for Cokes. Show you are one of them. Perhaps there are too many for you to be friendly with all of them, but cover those you can. Let them know you are one of them, that you belong, that you want to be accepted. Cultivate habits that make them want you to be with them, to include you in the parties, the fishing trips and such. Hold up your end financially, pay your share, buy the drink when it is your turn. Friendship with these fellows makes your job easier to handle. Of course, you'll run into leeches who try to milk you without offering anything in return. Drop these men. If they have little to offer you, they probably have little to offer the company. And you're not running too much risk that the "all for me" man will ever be your boss.

Select your close friends

You can't be buddy-buddy with all of the men at your level. But you can select two or three that you can make your close friends. One of the questions asked about a man up for promotion is, "Who are his friends?" Get friends that have the same interests, backgrounds, ambitions. Those you pegged as comers when you analyzed the competition. Then the king-makers can say, "He seems to be friendly with the right men." Not, "He buddies around with Poochie, the clown. How can he stand that character?" You and your wife may have more fun with Poochie and Mrs. P., but Pooch doesn't help build your image. Pair off with these men you select and their families, play bridge with them, go on picnics with them. Association with the right people may be more important in the small town than in the big city. In the small town you operate under everybody's eye. If you go around with the right kind of people, the kind that don't have the police out to stop loud parties, it is assumed you must be all right. Your friends may not be as interesting or as stimulating but they won't help you get blackballed.

Cooperate

Show you are willing to help the men at your level with advice and suggestions. If they ask you to do something that calls for you or your help to do a lot of work, explain your problem. Say, "Bert, you got fifty companies on this list. We'd have to dig out the folder on each one of the fifty and look up the information you want. If you have to have the information, we could show you where the folders are and then one of your men could dig them out and get the information." What you say here shows that you do not have the help to do the job but you are willing to cooperate. You didn't tell him you couldn't do it because you didn't have the help. You're still OK with him. If he wants to do the job as you suggest, he can do it but, if he doesn't have the help, he may find that he doesn't need the information as much as he thought he did. But you didn't turn him down. You showed yourself ready and willing.

Try out your ideas on them

Tell them about the project you are working on. Ask for their comments. You'll get ideas from them and you will confirm your thinking about certain points. You'll learn too about each man. One fellow will tell you that he is scared to death of an idea. What does he mean? Is he one that can make himself clear? Or is he one that doesn't want to commit himself? Another will give you reasons why it won't work. Is he negative on any kind of change? A third will be enthused about the idea. Is the idea that good or is he putting you on?

Work up courses with them

You need greater skill in public speaking so you organize a course in that subject. You hire an instructor or teach the course yourself. This studying together is a good mixing agent. I asked one supervisor, "You a friend of Wally over in the B aisle?" He replied, "Yeah, we studied economics together." If you teach the course, you learn more than the ones who take it. Not long ago I asked a supervisor who had taught a foundry course in a company, "Who learned the most in this course?" "I did," he said, "but we operate three types of foundries. I felt I should know more about them." Anytime that man's name comes up for promotion, the power will say, "He's the guy that organized that course in foundry practice."

Be interested in his problems

Louie is trying out a new kind of metal in his department. He tells you about it. Listen to what he says, ask questions to show your interest. This is Louie's idea. He sold it to his boss and to the engineers. When he tells you about it, he wants your questions. Your answers confirm his thinking, give him material that he can use with his superiors. Show an interest in his personal problems too. The youngster that is in the hospital, the new house he is building, the hobby he has taken up. If you get interested in his problems, he becomes interested in you.

Avoid retaliation

If someone doesn't want to cooperate with you, don't say, "I'll get even with him, just wait." Such an attitude doesn't hurt him as much as it hurts you. If one of the men at your level shows that he doesn't want to give you information you ask for, your natural inclination might be to remind him that you won't do something for him. But hold it. You may get a kick out of telling him off, but that doesn't help anybody, and the most important casualty is the company. Keep in mind, when working with a man at your level, you can help him and he can help you. You trade your help for his help. Don't change your method because one of these individuals is antagonistic, or vicious, or stupid. Heap coals of fire on him by working with him as if he were your best friend.

SELL THOSE BELOW YOU TOO

Abraham Lincoln said, "The Lord must have loved little people, he made so many of them." You have many of these little people around the office and they can help make the job you do more successful. A sales manager told me about one of his salesmen who was having trouble with shipments to his retailer customers. Other salesmen seemed to be having no such trouble. The sales manager investigated and found that the salesman with the trouble had been feuding with the shipping department. "Not exactly feuding," the sales manager explained, "but he was high-hatting them, ordering them around, complaining about them. And what did he gain? They started to sabotage him."

As you look about the office you see scores of little people who affect the job you do. You have to work with them, cooperate with them, get them on your side. Every one of those little people is a human being. And as such you know these things about him:

He feels that what he does is important.

He wants somebody to listen to him.

He likes a fellow who is courteous to him.

He doesn't like to be told to do things.

He wants to express his opinion.

He likes to do things his way.

He wants to stick to his routine.

He doesn't like changes.

He doesn't need any extra work.

You may have other information on some individuals, but the nine things mentioned apply to all of us. Then why not use this knowledge? The man who does has a better chance of getting what he wants.

Let him know he is important. Let's say you have asked the accounting for some information. The boss man sends you to Waldo, tells you Waldo will get it for you. Let's assume you don't know Waldo. He doesn't know you. You go to Waldo and say, "They tell me you're the top expert on. . . ." Waldo may say, "That sounds like you want something." But you didn't make him mad, did you? He may be only a clerk in a far-off corner of the office, but he is the expert on this information you want. The boss sent you and Waldo knows it. But the way you handled it shows that you think Waldo is important. He thinks he is, so why not agree with him?

Explain why you want the information. Waldo wants to be in on things. So bring him in. Explain that you are going to use this information to make up a presentation which your boss will make to the board of directors. Waldo begins to see how important your request is. These figures in his keeping are important enough to be presented to the board. He also sees that as the custodian of this information he is probably more important than he thought he was. Maybe it will take you two minutes to explain what you plan to do with the information, but it eases your problem in getting it quickly. Waldo has been bothered by a lot of hot shots who wanted information but told him nothing. By telling him you rate high in his book. Promise to tell him how the presentation to the board makes out. And follow through on that promise.

Ask his advice. Waldo wants to do things his way. You know the information is in file folders. Ask him what he thinks would be the best way to dig it out. You have an idea of how you want the information posted. You explain your plan, ask him if he feels that would be the best way. Don't argue about how he does it. His method may seem to be more difficult than the one you had in mind. Explain your way, but don't make a plea for it. Be satisfied with the way he wants to do it. He will be happier with his way. You want the information, not a discussion on methods.

Offer to help. This request of yours may call for some extra work by Waldo and you know he doesn't want any extra work. So offer to help. Say, "If you will show me where the folders are, I'll bring a man over and we'll dig it out." Note that this tells Waldo you are not too good to dig information out of folders and record it. When Waldo sees you are willing to do this, how can he help but have a better opinion of you?

Ask, don't tell. When you want information from another department, ask for it. Don't tell them that you have to have it, that they have to give it to you, that the big boss wants it right now. Ask what is the best way to get it, ask how they want to give it to you, ask how they can get it with the minimum of work, ask if you can help them dig it out. Ask, ask, ask. If you try to tell them anything, they can truthfully say, "You don't understand this problem." You may understand it better than they do, but don't take on the job of convincing them that you do.

Don't suggest changes. You may think that the way the accountants keep the figures is all wet, but don't bring that up. Both Waldo and his boss resist change. Act as if this way of theirs is the right way. There is no sense complicating your request for a few figures by a criticism of the handling of those figures. By suggesting a change the others get the idea that you are a wise guy that could do anything better. Suggest changes in your own department to your boss, but don't mention changes to the people who handle the work, or to the people in other departments.

Use common courtesy. I've said this before. When you ask anyone to do anything, use "please." When he does it, thank him for what he has done. When Waldo gives you the figures on a typed sheet, compliment him on how quickly he did it. Common courtesy can do a lot to build your image around the office.

Remember people. Perhaps you will have just one opportunity to work with Waldo in five years. But remember him. When you see him in the cafeteria, greet him. If you know he is a bowler, ask how his game is. You were friendly to Waldo when you wanted something from him. Keep on being friendly. You may want something from him again.

Snub not the boss's secretary

This gal can make you or break you. I'd suggest you make a study of the secretaries that you have to contact. But first, understand the importance of these women. The jokers put it, "The boss has a wife to tell him what to do and a secretary to get it done." There is a lot of truth in this. She is the only one around the office that can order the boss around. And a good secretary moves in and does this too. Ever been around when the boss's secretary quits and a new girl tries to take her place? She can't find anything, she doesn't know what telephone calls to put through, which men to let into the office. The boss is frustrated. And so the boss who has a secretary that operates a smoothly run outer office places someone between you and him that you had better understand. Her job, as far as you are concerned, is to get people into his office who should go in and keep people out who should stay out. She also has some checking to do to get data or reports from you.

In giving an indoctrination pitch to trainees who had just joined the company, I had a special speech on secretaries. We had a number of them and these young men had to contact the girls to get to see the boss men. I said, "These girls are important. The boss man depends on them. He has to back them up in any rhubarb. They are more important than you are. Perhaps you do have a college degree, maybe a master's, but, when it comes to the operation of the big man's office, those girls are smarter than you are. It won't do any good to try to impress these girls with your importance. They know how important you are. When you approach any secretary around the place, approach her just as you would her boss, with all the courtesy you would accord him. She's just a girl, sure, but she is important. If she likes you, she will help you. If she doesn't like you, you are out."

Here are some suggestions for approaching her as if she were the boss.

Ask for help and advice. Let's say you approach her, "I want to see the boss." She says, "There are a number ahead of you." You ask, "How long will it be?" She says, "I can't tell you, for I don't know how long these others need." So your name goes on the list. And your approach didn't show much of an appreciation of her job. Let's say you asked her, "When do you think you can get me in?" This question puts her in the picture, asks for a decision from her. It implies she can find a time. Further, it makes her the important one. You are not asking to see the boss, you are asking her to set a time. Another approach is, "How is his schedule today?" His schedule is her business. She says, "Rather full." You say, "Maybe I better come back tomorrow." She may say, "Oh, it's not that bad." You have given her a choice and she will try to run you in.

Don't telephone for appointments. It is easier to turn down a telephone request for an appointment. Walk over to her office, the exercise will do you good. You're there now and she might say, "He's in there now. Why don't you go right in." Usually she will add, "He's got a meeting in ten minutes." That's to speed you up. Remember that she is the custodian of Mr. Big's time.

Don't try to snoop. Her office may be a great place to pick up information but don't use it as such. When you are in her office, walk out when she takes a telephone call. Don't try to look at letters or papers on her desk. Don't ask her questions about matters that are none of your business. These things are dishonest and may cause her to think, "You have to watch this boy." One of her jobs is to protect her boss from snoopers.

Don't try to kid her. She knows the score, perhaps lots better than you do. You tell her, "The boss said he wanted to see me." Just this morning he had told her, "Don't let that monkey in to see me. I know what he wants." You have made capital with that one, haven't you?

Explain what you want. At times it may help to tell her what you want. Perhaps you have to have a decision on this purchase today. Tomorrow the price goes up. Perhaps all you need is a "yes" or "no," if you could break in for just a minute. She might be able to arrange that. But let her make the decision about whether or not she should try.

Suggest, don't order. Ask, "Could you do this for me?" You are not telling her, you are suggesting. A man who goes to the secretary and tells how important he is and his deal is and why the boss would want to hear about it now makes no headway at all. Remember she knows more about what the boss wants than you do.

Don't underestimate the girls. Once, when a department manager was looking for a man, I suggested one trainee. "I don't want that man," he said. "I've been checking on him."

"What do you mean checking?" I asked.

"With the secretaries," he answered. "They say he's a no-good."

"He been making passes at them?" I asked.

"No, not that. It's the way he treats them, like dirt. He thinks he is so much better than they are."

"We can correct that. I'll give him a talking to."

"Yeah, you do that but count me out. I don't want a guy in my department too stupid to get along with the dames around here."

I'd suggest you treat any of the girls around the place as equals and treat the secretaries of the bosses as you would their bosses.

Ring the doorbells

Working with the others around the office is much like the candidate for public office, ringing doorbells. You make contacts and you talk to people. In business you are ringing those doorbells everyday. You are spreading the news that you are a good and competent Joe.

Think of these methods:

1. Cultivate the people around you in the company in such a way that you do two things; one, get the work done, and two, leave a good impression of you.

2. Contact the top executives in a way that demonstrates your competence.

3. Work with executives at your level in a way that builds friends and helps both you and them.

4. Contact the little people in a way that helps them rate you as a good Joe.

5. Handle the secretaries of the big shots so they are on your side.

Let's assume all this study, work and effort, plus a little bit of luck, has brought you a promotion—what now?

13

Start Right on the New Job

Hooray!

You got the bigger job.

Congratulations.

Perhaps it's only a straw-boss job, but you moved up. Now you're in the position of the young ballplayer that just came up to the big league. When asked how he liked it, he said, "Fine, but there are so many people watching you."

Everybody is watching you now. They shake your hand and wish you well. But inwardly they may be asking, "How lucky can you get?" or "It will be interesting to see how he makes out." Everybody is in on this watching. Those above, those at your level, and the ones below you. The big spot is on you. Thus you want to start right, to make that good first impression.

Impress those above and those below

Some experts will tell you, "Impress those below and you impress those at the top." That may be true, but you are just starting on this job. You want to make a good impression on everybody. I once heard an executive say, "It's not fair to that fellow to put him on that job. He hasn't got what it takes to swing it." Some will feel that way about you, others will hope you do well. Some couldn't care less and some are hoping you fall flat.

But all are watching, ready to boo or applaud. Thus how you start will be of interest to everybody.

START RIGHT WITH THOSE ABOVE YOU

This group selected you. They gave you the job. They want you to succeed because if you fail they have to make another change, and changes are a headache always. You appeared to be the best bet, and so they selected you. To get off right with them, you might:

Be modest

Don't indicate to those above you that you feel this new job will be a breeze. Talk about it as a challenge, one you have tried to train for. Let them know that you can't do it all alone, that you need their help and the help of your employees. Any step upward is a tough adjustment. You can make it, surely, but it will take work and training and you need help. Show this in your manner and in what you say.

Ask for advice

By asking for advice from the man ahead of you, you show you don't know it all, you want to keep from making some mistakes that a new boss might make. You might ask, "I want to get started right on this job and show that you were right in recommending me. Can you think of any mistakes I shouldn't make?" Ask also for advice about personnel. Which will resent your taking over, which will go along with you just as they did with him. Which have to be needled, which complimented? A man moving off a job wants to feel that his special know-how can be helpful. While he is being moved up, he still feels a proprietorship in the old job, in the group that he has trained. Thus he is willing to help. Start getting this advice when you first know you are going to take over.

If the man whose job you took over is not available for contact, go to the man who is now your boss. Perhaps he had to fire the boss whose job you took. OK, have him tell you about the mistakes that led him to get rid of the man. It could be mighty easy to make some of those same mistakes. Then too he may want you to do some things about shifting employees, letting them go, changing their assignments. You want to know this.

If your old boss retired or moved up, continue to ask for his advice in the weeks that follow. Call on him at least once each month and let him know how things are going. Always ask for his suggestions. You don't have to follow them, but by getting them and talking them out, you can help straighten out your own thinking about the job and the department. This man before you has had experience in talking with those above him. He has been thinking like a manager for a long period. You want to learn how to think like a manager. Before you talked to him as employee to manager, now you speak to him as manager to manager. There's a difference. So keep in touch. Ask for advice, help, suggestions.

Discuss what you need

Now that you have taken over this job, ask the boss above what he feels you need to make a success of this new opportunity. It may be a change in thinking, in habits, some training. In discussing you for this job, those above talked over your strengths and weaknesses. You know they did this, for this is common management practice. Thus your weaknesses are fresh in the mind of your boss. If you feel you are weak in certain skills, ask the man above if he agrees. If he does, ask what he suggests you do to correct this weakness.

Read more. You are no doubt weak in the reading you do. Most of us are. Last week I heard a speaker, the head of a corporation, say, "Every executive should read one book on management each month." After his speech I asked him, "Do the executives of your company read one book on management per month?"

"Are you kidding?" he laughed. "If they did," he added, "I'd have a better management team."

There is no doubt of this. Check back on what you have read on management in the past year. If your score is zero, don't despair, you have lots of company. Most of your competitors don't read either. But you are interested in you not in those competitors. Let them take care of themselves. B. C. Forbes said, "The man who has no time to read about business, has no time to succeed in business."

You may say, "But many of the men above don't read." That's true, they don't. It is why you have a plus if you read. One executive made this crack, "Why surrender yourself to self-imposed ignorance?" Read and you come up with more ideas than the fellow who never cracks a book.

What should you read? Ask others about this. Read about the skills you need. Training is a continuous job. You trained yourself to get this one, now you need training to hold it. You'll need further training to get and hold the job up ahead. Let the men above know that you are willing to train yourself.

Don't overwhelm the boss with your problems

You show the boss that you are running scared when you bring every problem to him. You may feel that you are new on the job and, to play it safe, you better get his OK before you act. But he put you on the job to run the job, not because he wanted to make your decisions for you.

Talk out any fast changes

If you are called on to make any changes early in your regime, talk them out with those above you. Make sure they understand what you are trying to do. You know what happens when you make a change in personnel. Andy, the victim, goes to somebody up above with whom he has an in and says, "That so-and-so just fired me."

"We'll see about that," the big shot says. And so the story about you firing Andy starts around in management circles. When it gets back to your boss, if he has been informed, he says, "Oh, yes, we agreed on that." And perhaps he is able to set the big man straight. You offered Andy two other jobs and he wouldn't take them. Andy didn't mention that. Andy has a lousy record on attendance. He didn't mention that. But you are protected by the man who should protect you, your boss.

A change in procedure can cause turmoil out of all proportion to what the change means. You know that all of us resist change. The change may make the worker's job easier, but it is new and they are afraid of anything new. On any proposed change work out a list of advantages and disadvantages and discuss these with the boss. If you feel that your group is going to complain to the union steward or to him, let him know that they will. If he is completely informed he will be prepared when the rhubarb starts.

START WELL WITH THOSE BELOW

Not long ago a man I had worked with years ago was made the general manager of a company. I heard from friends who worked for him, "This guy is an SOB." He wasn't that type at all when I knew him and so I asked one of his group, "Is it true what I hear that this guy is an SOB?"

"Yeah, one of the most proficient," he admitted.

"I can't understand it," I said. "He was a nice guy when I worked with him."

"Let's face it, Ed. When he got this big job, he felt he had to attract attention and one certain way is to be an SOB, right?"

It is, of course. It may attract favorable attention from the men above but it makes a lot of enemies below. It may be that he was hired to be an SOB.

Another manager took over a division of a company. When

I asked how he was doing, one of his men said, "He spends most of his time patting people on the back, telling them how well they are doing." This course is bound to make friends down below but what will it do with the men up above?

Unless he has been selected to follow a certain course, the choice to a new supervisor is his. He can be a good guy or bad guy. I'm not advising which course to follow, but I do offer these suggestions for making a good impression on those below:

Ask for help

Approach the new duties with a humility that shows those around you that you can't do it all yourself, that you need their help. You can emphasize this attitude with those below you more than you can with those above. The fellow below can picture himself suddenly pushed into your new job. He might wonder whether or not he could handle it. The one above may think you lack confidence.

When one of your employees congratulates you, say, "Thanks, Chuck, I'll need your help. You know that, don't you?" Discuss your new setup on the basis, "We got a lot of hard work ahead of us." This is a project. You are the leader, yes, but they are needed too. Let them know that they are.

Get the group together

Get the group together and ask for their cooperation, the same kind of loyalty they gave the old boss. Tell them that perhaps one of the others might have been more competent for the job, or just as competent, but management selected you. Explain that you have a lot to learn and you want them to help you, that you don't understand all the details of each man's work. This is a most important meeting so plan it well. Figure out the questions that might be asked and answer them as well as possible. Your objective is to get the group with you. When a fellow from another department asks, "What do you think of your new boss?" you want the right answer from your employee. If your man says, "OK," the fellow from the other department will go back and tell his boss, "The fellows like him." Explain that, if any of them have ideas about how the work can be improved, you will listen to their ideas. Tell them that they all did a good job for the old boss and you hope that they will do as well for you.

Talk out with competition

Perhaps one or two of the men in the department were considered for the job you now hold. They may think that they should have had the job instead of you. They may feel that you are incompetent. If they were considered for the job, they are probably men you want to keep. Perhaps they are already looking for new jobs. Recognize this situation. Get these men into your office one by one and talk to them frankly about how they feel. Ask such questions as, "Why do you think they selected me?" If you know why the man didn't get the promotion, ask some questions about the weakness that dealt him out. Explain that you do not know the workings of their departments. Discuss personnel with them. Ask which man each is training to take over when he is promoted. Assure him that you are his friend, that you will do anything you can to help him get what he wants in the company. If possible, arrange a salary increase for him. This will make it tougher for him to take another job.

These talks won't always be pleasant and they won't always

be a success, but it is better to talk about how the man feels and make sure that you understand one another.

There's going to be some changes made

Don't start off with such an announcement. Perhaps there are some changes you will have to make but keep quiet about them. What are you saying about your old boss when you announce, "We're going to do things differently?" You are saying he wasn't doing it right. And he has gone up. He says, "Oh, the guy can do it better than I can." So you lose one friend. Then think of the effect on the help. They ask, "What's he have in mind?" And so you start rumors, some good men may start looking for new jobs. You may have to make changes. Perhaps the old boss laughed when you were appointed and told you, "I'm glad you have to make those changes instead of me." Then too the new boss up above may have instructed you to make the changes. He may have said, "Charlie was too soft-hearted to fire that guy." Still, don't sound off needlessly.

Don't tell all

In the new job you'll have access to information that you did not have in the job below. You'll be tempted to talk about this for it shows how you stand with those above. But hold up. You may believe in a policy of keeping everybody informed, but there are some things that it is best to keep to yourself. If you learn of future plans, it may be better to keep them under your hat until they are about ready to go. You might let your key men know that you are working on something. But do this only if it will help. In holding up information, don't make remarks that cause the listeners to wonder what is in the works. This may be worse than telling it all. For now they begin to discuss what is coming. If it is information that is bound to leak out, try to make sure that it comes first from you.

Don't adopt a management vocabulary

In time you may get to this, heaven forbid. But don't start with it. I mean those words like "implement" and "integrate" that you find in management magazines. If you suddenly adopt such jargon, the others will think that the new appointment has gone to your head. And what's more important, they won't understand you.

Be alert for any drop in interest

It would be quite natural for a department to goof off under a new boss, to check on what it can get away with. Watch for this. Under the old boss, the department turned out so many units of work, check to see that you don't drop below that total. If you are slipping some, check on why. Are the workers taking advantage of the new boss? How are they doing it? What about morale? Absenteeism? These problems may not be the important ones in your department but check the important ones to you. I mention them to show the types of problems to check. Remember somebody up above is checking. You have to keep up with the old records and better them if you are to attract the attention of the men above.

Handle old friends diplomatically

One of the tough decisions to make when you move up even one notch is what to do about old friends. You went to

lunch with Poochie every day. But now you may be expected
to go to lunch with men at your new level. You may be entitled to eat at the executives' table in the cafeteria, or in the
executive dining room. Go along with what the job calls for.
You may not want to lose Poochie as a pal, but you are planning to move up too. Try to handle Poochie and other such
situations your new status brings up without losing the
friends.

Watch evidence of new affluence

Don't start wearing your Sunday suit the first day on the
job. Don't show up in a newer and bigger car the second day.
Maybe you needed a new car and were going to buy it anyway but rattle along in the old one for a few months yet. This
may be bad advice for the nation's economy, but it is good
politics for you. Don't buy the big house right away or join
the country club. Wait awhile. Give the people under you an
opportunity to get accustomed to the idea that you are a boss
before you start spending the few bucks extra you find on your
paycheck.

Move in on the poachers

You're new on the job and it is quite natural that another
department head may move in on your authority. At the first
sign of such poaching, go into action. Tell the man that this
is yours and that he is to keep hands off. It may be a part of
your work that he has wanted for years. In that time he may
have built up some good reasons why he should have that
work. If he persists, go to the boss and have it out with him.
Work up a good case before you go in screaming. The boss

may ask, "Why shouldn't he have it?" Be prepared to answer that question. If one fellow gets away with some of your preserve, others may try to nick off other bits. So keep your eyes open. If the boss sees that these others can impose on you, he won't think too highly of you. Why should he think highly of a fellow that can be pushed around?

Learn the jobs

If there is a variety of work done in the department and you have had little contact with some of it, bring yourself up to date on these jobs. Have the men holding the jobs explain the work. Set aside enough time so that you can talk about the man's job as much as he wants to talk about it. The discussion will help bring you up to date on his work, and it will show him that his work is important to you. It is highly probable that no other boss ever spent this much time talking to him about his problems.

Use "We" not "I"

When you use the capital "I," you sound as if you are bragging, that you are a wise guy, that you know it all. Give the other fellow credit. Learn to say instead, "We want this," "The department wants this," "The company wants this." When the department does something, give the credit to them. Not, "My policy is...," instead, "The department's policy is...." Instead of "I would like to tell you...," say, "You'll be interested to hear...." Instead of saying, "This is my opinion," say, "Isn't this your opinion?" The "we" and "you" gives credit to the other fellow. Maybe you did do the job, but somebody helped, didn't they? OK, give them a share of the credit.

Tell me you know all this

Most executives do. That gives me the opportunity to ask, "Fine, how much of it are you using?" For it is not what you know that is important. You make your record on what you use of what you know. Check back through this advice and ask yourself, "How much of it am I using?" You want to start right on this new job. OK, use all you know to get off to that right start.

The right start helps

Perhaps you will be on this job a long time, but your record in those first few months helps you a lot. Fumble the start and you raise doubts. You are like the ballplayer again. Stumble on the way down to first base when you are dragging a bunt and you may get thrown out. So plan for the right start. With a right start, you haven't got it made. But you have eliminated some possible trouble. Here is a review of the advice in this chapter.

1. The right start is important because everybody is watching. If you are going to rise in the company, you need as many boosters as you can make.

2. Your audience is those above you, those at your level, and those below. Think of all of them.

3. Those above you will want you to succeed. They put you on this job. Ask their help and advice.

4. Impress those below you that you mean business. That their work is important and that you will work together to attain the goals set.

Now that you are off to a good start, let's see how you can build this group of yours into a good team.

14

Know and Build Your Team

Now it is your team.

Under the old boss, it was his team.

It may have been good, bad, indifferent. But even if it was the best possible, it can fold up completely under a new manager. And, of course, it can perk up.

You want the latter and it will pay you to:

First, check on what you have, and

Second, build up the group's morale.

CHECK ON WHAT YOU HAVE

At the ballpark, the fellow selling scorecards calls, "You can't tell the players without a scorecard." You'll be a smart manager if you make a rather complete scorecard on every employee in this group of yours.

Recently I told a young man who had been put on his first managerial job, "The new job should be a challenge to you."

He answered, "You said it. You should see the men I got assigned to me."

I asked, "Have you checked their abilities?"

"That's what discourages me," he said. "But that is a part of management, isn't it, taking a gang like that and getting it shaped up?"

It is a part of management. And for the new manager who wants to get ahead, it is an important part of management. Find out what you've got, what you can do with what you've got, how what you've got can help you make the record you need to move up the ladder. You might try these ideas:

Make a list of the key men

List each of the key men and analyze each on the six factors you used to rate yourself: ability, image, health, attitude, conformity, honesty. Let's assume you may have taken over a department with forty men. Out of such a group you will probably have four or five key men. Start with these first. You may say, "But I got only three men and a girl in the department." OK, list them. I'd suggest that you make a separate sheet on each man. You may have them listed on a payroll sheet or in a little black book, but make separate sheets for each, one for Artie, one for Bertie, and so on. Start with a separate sheet on each key man.

Fill in the sheets

At the left-hand side of the sheet on Artie, write the six factors mentioned:

Ability

Image

Health

Attitude

Conformity

Education and experience

Motivation

Space the factors so that you have some blank space to write about each. Now start writing what you know about the men under these headings. You'll find that you have two types of men; one, those that are satisfied to stay where they are and two, those that want to get ahead. But all that tell you they are ambitious to get ahead aren't willing to work to prove it. Some will say, "I'm willing to work from 9 to 5 and, if that will make it, fine." To others, hours of work mean nothing. You won't be able to fill in all of this data in your first go around with the sheets. This is a job you will work at perhaps over a period of months but get as much down on paper as you can right now. Start with your list and a sheet on each key man. Then to help in your analysis of men and jobs you might use these mechanical devices——

The job description. Let's say each man on your list does a different job. What does that job call for? If you asked the man, he might say, "I'm a billing clerk." Your next question was, "OK, just exactly what do you do?" He might have to fumble a bit to come up with the right answer. If your company has job descriptions, get these out and refresh yourself on the duties called for by each job. If you don't have such descriptions, make up your own. Here is an outline for a job description:

1. Name of job

2. What the worker does

3. What he should know—education, special training, ex-perience

4. Skills he needs, knowledge in certain phases

5. Tools he uses

6. Conditions of his work

If you will fill in the information under each of these headings, you will have a fair description of most jobs. If you have to make up job descriptions, you might have the man on the job help you. Give him the outline and let him write his own job description. You write one too and then discuss the two. He is more likely to go along with a job description that he has helped make up.

Now a man specification. With the job spelled out, you can now work up a man spec that puts down on paper what it takes to hold the job successfully. Most man specifications cover these phases:

1. Physical

2. Educational

3. Experience

4. Aptitudes and ability

5. Personality

You might have the man on the job help you with these man specifications, just as he did with the job description. In this you will have to check the results because the man is almost certain to describe his own qualifications as those best fitted for the job. For instance, he may state that a man is needed. Some study may show that a woman could handle the job. He may say a college graduate or equivalent, when a high school graduate with some special training could handle the job well. Discuss all of these points with him and arrive at a specification that you feel is nearer the facts. Now with a job description for each job and a man spec for it, you can——

Study the assignments

Charlie's job calls for a knowledge of engineering, yet Charlie has no engineering training. As a result he has to spend some of his time with the engineers to get the answers to questions that his job spec says that he should know. On less complicated jobs you can easily see that a man who has to talk to customers on the telephone should be one who likes to talk to people on the telephone and has some facility at it, or a man who has to meet customers should have a personality that wears well with those customers he meets. As you study these assignments and the men handling them, you know that you are not going to immediately transfer a man because he does not exactly fit the job. But, if a man doesn't fit the job, he has certain limitations that tell you you have to watch this job more closely and may have to move in and help him on occasions. If assignments are not the best, you may have to move men, shift them to other jobs or other departments.

Measure the job knowledge

The man on the job may know all about the mailing-list stencils, how they are made and how they are changed, and he may be able to run the addressing machine. But what does he know about the purpose of his job, about the company, the industry, the product or service? Will such knowledge help him? To get the men in the factory to understand what one of their mistakes meant to a customer, one company put on a campaign that asked the men, "How would your wife feel if she got one of our products without handles?" If it will help your group to know what the shooting is for, ask yourself how you can get this information to them.

How about incentive?

Some of your men may have no real incentive and you may have to manufacture incentives for them. Others are so engrossed in their jobs that the work itself is adequate incentive to keep them humping. One man told me, "I can't wait to get in in the morning. I never know what's going to happen." Find out what is motivating each man in your department. Ask him about it. It is not always money. For those with no real incentive, make some suggestions. Some of your men may never have thought of promotion. If you mention the possibility, they may work for it. You will show up as a better supervisor if you find out what will make your men run.

What training is needed?

As you check these men of yours and their jobs, you'll find that some of them need training to better handle the assignments they now have and training to handle other jobs that they might take on. Make a list of the training you feel is needed by each key man. Discuss this with the man and see how he feels about it. If he is willing to take the training, work out a plan for him to get it.

Start looking for your successor

Now while you are studying your personnel, start thinking of your successor. You may say, "Whoa, I'm not even started myself yet." That's true, but it is not too early. Supposing a better job came up tomorrow. The higher-ups might say, "We just got Tom started on that new job and so we can't consider him." It is unlikely that the new job might come up so soon, but supposing it came up in two months. At that time one of the higher-ups asked you, "We got a job that you would fit into. You got anybody down there that could take over for you?" It would be good to have a name to suggest, wouldn't it? Perhaps you have one or two men that could be moved in, but, if you don't have a candidate, get out the personnel records and check on the possibilities. Interview those you think have training or might be trained to take over. If you have no possibilities in your group, look about the company for a man who has, or check the personnel department. Management finds it much easier to move you up to a better job if you have somebody to take over.

Look at the general picture

This analysis of what you have to work with will give you a new look at management problems. You'll find that as you advance in management you'll see less of the detail and more of the overall picture. You'll find that, in addition to working to turn in good jobs, other managers at your level are studying their groups. Your boss is studying the men at your level. His boss is studying the men at the level above that. I don't mean that you are not now interested in details. You are, of course. You check them as you always did. But the details are not all, and now you have an interest in that all—the details plus.

Know your team

I suggested that you make a separate sheet on each of your key men. Take the sheet on Artie home tonight, and, when you get a few minutes, study it. Study the statistics on him. Think about what he is good at, where he can improve, what will stimulate him to improve. Give Artie a thorough going-over. Tomorrow night take home the information you have on Bertie. Continue this until you have all the men studied. In time you will have a fairly good picture of this team of yours. In making the checks suggested, talk to these men. These talks will be the greatest help you have. Of one thing you can be certain, any time you spend studying your team won't be wasted. For this is your team, your clique, the gang that's with you, a good thing to have in any kind of politics.

Root for your team

This study does one other thing for you. It gives you data that helps you root for your team. You know Jack better now. You know more about his good points, and, when anyone asks about Jack or his work, you can stress the good points. I have a friend who jokingly says, "He's a relative. He's got to be good." This is the attitude you should have to your group. They have good points, and you can tell others what they are. So boost your group, talk about the good jobs they do and the records they make.

BUILD THE GROUP'S MORALE

One way is to let them know that you feel this way about them. For morale just doesn't happen. You have to do something about it. Let's say a department has a high morale. You ask one of the group why. It's highly probable that he'll say, "The boss is a good guy, he is for us, lets us in on things."

"An easy guy to work for?" you ask.

"No, I can't say that. He keeps on you but he backs you up 100 per cent."

Once you know the individuals that make up your team, it will be easier to use the devices in the list that follows to build their morale. Each has been mentioned in the pages before, and each can help you weld this group into a team. Here they are:

1. *Communication.* Keep your group informed on what is going on, results, current activities, future prospects. Move in on rumors. Check on indoctrination, knowledge of fringe benefits. Your employee likes to think that he is in on the know.

2. *Your meetings.* These help build the idea that you are all working together for the same end. Hold meetings regularly, give the employees a part, use visuals, let them have their say.

3. *Work practices.* Be courteous. They all want to feel that what they do is important in the overall operation of the company. Show them why they are important.

4. *Status symbols.* We all want recognition, the pat on the back for a job well done, the name on the office door. Learn to give credit where it is due.

5. *Listening.* This part of communication is so important that it rates a tool in itself. Hear what the employee says, let him know that you heard, and show an interest.

6. *Counseling.* This is one of the most helpful tools you have in getting the employee to feel that he is on your side. Use it.

Follow this plan in studying and building your team:

1. Know your men, know what they can do and can't do.
2. Use the mechanical devices such as job description and

man specification to see if you are making the best use of what talent you have.

3. Remember that one of the functions of an executive is training. If your men need training, suggest it and help them to get it.

4. Start looking for a successor in your group. Think of grooming him to take over.

5. Work for a high morale, a group that feels it is a team, your team.

6. Root for your team always, just as you would for your company or product.

Now that you know your team, what about the job ahead?

15

Keep an Eye on the Next Promotion

You haven't made it yet. You have moved up just one step. Maybe you skipped a grade and that is wonderful, but there are jobs up ahead to plan for.

Start planning now

Things have changed. The possibilities ahead have changed, your competition has toughened. Different boys are wielding the hatchets. Complications have come up. If you want to keep on climbing, make another check on your chances. Here are some thoughts:

List the jobs ahead

List all of the jobs above your level. Now look at the list and cross off those that are not open to you because of the technical know-how needed. For instance, if you don't happen to be an engineer or accountant, engineering and accounting may have to go. Next cross off those you don't want because they are dead ends. Let's say you are head of a department now. Another department is responsible for twice the business yours is. The other department might be a better spot than yours. List it too. Don't kid yourself on this. Aim your sights at the possible.

Determine the logical moves upward

Crumley, the head of a department, is about to retire. He has not built up an assistant. Somebody outside the department is going to get the job. Why not you? Analyze each possibility ahead like this one of Crumley's. Which jobs might possibly be open in the near future? Which jobs have a backup man that is the logical successor? Some jobs up there are more possible for you than others. Which jobs are they?

Analyze the new competition

Next make a list of the men who are now at your new level. Rate them as you think the boss might on their possibilities for promotion. Some you can rule out completely because of age, health, ambition, and other factors. But analyze carefully the ones that you feel will offer real competition to you. What have they got? What don't they have? How do they stand politically?

Boost your successor

I suggested you needed a successor to take over when you move up. When you select one, build him up. Here are ideas:

Sell him to the boss on every occasion.

Train him to take over. Check him continuously to see that he is learning.

Give him opportunities to impress the power—send him on important contacts, take him to meetings, give him spots on meetings, have him present ideas.

When the power realizes this man is ready to take over for you, they know you are available to move up.

Look for ideas

Most of us are not creative, but the man who comes up with ideas attracts management's attention. Most such ideas come from reading or from contact with other executives at management club meetings. If you hear that over at the Cjax plant a new idea is being tried out, don't say, "That won't work for us." Ask instead, "Could I adapt that and use it?" If you feel you can, this may mean going to the Cjax plant, studying the operation, perhaps bringing your superiors there to see for themselves. But do the necessary, work up your cost and savings figures. Then present the completed plan to your boss and those above who must approve. This type of activity shows that you are alive, alert, willing to try new ideas. In most companies a man who has these qualities is considered a comer.

Think of the creative route

In looking for a place to move up, think of making your own job. This is a possibility that might not occur to you. I have seen men plan an activity they felt would help the company. They worked out plans for the activity and then sold management on setting up the activity with the originator as the manager. To do this a man had to know the company and particularly its weaknesses. Here is an example, perhaps too simple. The company is weak on service to customers. Management knows this, but nobody has done anything about it. Now this operator comes up with a plan to give this service that is lacking. He suggests setting up a new department to handle it. He presents the plan to his boss, and then to those above. The operator did the research, collected the data on costs and savings, and prepared himself to answer all questions. He showed the company how it could make money or build good will by following his plan. His plan is accepted and he is put in charge. You might say that he promoted himself.

Look around for such ideas. They might come from a move a competitor makes, a diversification of product, the addition of a new product, a change in the needs of certain customers, a development in another industry. Ask yourself, "What does the company need?"

This type of plan calls for a knowledge of the business and an awareness of what is happening in your industry and the industries of your company's customers. But it does offer possibilities. I talked to one able executive who was on a dead-end job and knew he was on his way out. He developed such an activity, was put in charge of it, and is back in the thick of competition again.

Think what this type of project does for you. It stamps you as a thinker, a man with ideas, a planner, one who is interested in the company. And, if you handle the activity successfully, you are the man who had the idea, organized it, got it off the ground, and moved to accomplish the objective for which it was created.

Some may say, "Things like that couldn't happen in our company." OK, look around you. How many of the departments in the business were operating five years ago? If there are new ones, ask why they were started. Then ask, "Who had the original idea for starting that department?"

Let's assume your attempt to sell the idea is a failure. You developed it, presented it, but did not put it over. Well, you have had a favorable exposure, haven't you? If your presentation was good, it impressed somebody up above, and that impression will be remembered when you are considered for promotion. I don't suggest that you consider failure when you present such a project. But, if you do well in presenting the idea, it is mighty difficult for you to lose.

If you succeed, get your own business, and operate it successfully, you prove yourself the kind of executive that most companies want. I'd suggest you look for this type of opportunity. Study each new development in technology, industry practice, or methods, and you may come up with what you want.

Keep your plans up-to-date

Let's say that your original plans called for moving up to Old Crumley's job. But Crumley retired and you didn't get that. OK, what is your plan now? Perhaps Maddy had a man groomed as his successor and the boss stole him for another assignment. How about that spot? Keep on planning or you may be left behind. Aim at the new job, continue to train yourself to hold that higher job.

Assess what has happened to you

When you moved onto this supervisory job, you became a manager. Perhaps you are at the lowest level of management in your company. But you are a part of management now, and that changes your image in the eyes of many people. On the plus side this means:

a. You are in a new spotlight. You get more recognition because you can broadcast your image to more people who count.

b. You are more important to the people watching you, those above and those below. Those above may say, "We need more men like him." Competition may say, "I'll have to watch that guy, he may rough up my plans."

c. You'll have more contact with big shots. In time they will accept you as a fellow big shot.

On the negative side this means:

a. You'll have to give more time to the job, take work home, see less of the wife and family, play less golf, spend more time reading and studying to get equipped for that job ahead.

b. Some social activities that you enjoy will have to be passed up. You'll have to listen to the wife's complaints about a husband who is married to his job.

c. Old friends may have to be pushed aside, new friends made.

d. You'll have to conform more than you like, in dress, ideas, thoughts expressed. A statement out of line can mean more now.

e. You'll be asked to join intrigues that you may feel are not good for you or the company. Some may be designed to scuttle you.

f. Move carefully because more hatchets will be out to chop you down.

You trade something for something

Back in the early pages of this book, I said that you had to trade something for something. As you advance you'll have to give more and more of your freedom for what you want in the company. I'd suggest you ask yourself, "Can I take this in stride?" Well, you got this promotion, didn't you? You are a supervisor, part of management. Deliver more of the same and you will get higher supervisory jobs. In most cases they go to the man who is a success down below.

Keep the stars in sight

Your plans to get that job ahead should include:

1. Knowing what job you want
2. Getting and training an assistant to take over your job
3. Looking for ideas that will help the company and help you
4. Perhaps finding a company need that you can develop into a department of your own
5. Continuing your development and training
6. Keeping your plans up-to-date

It may seem a long way from your first supervisory job to the top jobs up ahead. But handle this first job well and you will get a better job on your next promotion, then a still better job on the promotion after that. Usually you go up one job at a time, one level at a time. Eventually after a number of these promotions, you'll get one of the really top jobs.

The next chapters deal with what to do then.

part 3

How to Hold onto the Top Job

Chapters 13 and 14 gave a number of suggestions for success in a supervisory job. Now let's assume that through the political machinations described in the preceding chapters plus ability, timing, marriage, luck, or any of the other factors that make for business success, you have at last arrived at a top job. Perhaps not the real top, but you are high, really high. In your setup you could be called— Number One, Mr. Big.

Congratulations!

But don't assume you are finished with company politics. As the top man you have to recognize that

a. *There is politics both above and below you.*

b. *This politics can harm or help both the company and you, and*

c. *Your job calls for accepting the responsibility to deal with this politics and the politicians.*

The following chapters offer suggestions given by high executives who have wrestled with company politics and have tried to curb it, promote it, turn it to an advantage.

16

What's So Different from up Here?

From the big office——

It doesn't look so different, does it?

But for you it is. You're the top man now, maybe the president, the executive V.P., the head of a division or a factory. In your setup, you are the works, the big shot, and also the big target.

The suggestions in the remaining chapters are written as if they apply to the top executive officer only, but they can be used by any highly placed executive. For politics goes on all around you.

Up above you, what about those members of the board or company officers that were outvoted in your selection? Could some of them be out to get you? The ones that were for you are hoping that they were right, but they don't plan to keep fighting for you. Perhaps they were more interested in winning the fight than in putting you on this job. Then, if you are the president and top executive officer, how about the chairman and vice-chairman, what ideas do they have?

Down below, company politics is eddying and swirling as usual. All through the company this question is being asked, "Kootsie's got the job. How do we get in good with Kootsie?" The next question is, "Can we handle him as easily as the guy before him?"

If you came up through the company, you know this. Just last month you were in this type of intrigue yourself. If you came from the outside or from another division, recognize these facts of life. The politickers will be working to gain your favor, snatch some or all of your power, nullify your policies, or to make it a bit more difficult for you to hang onto this job. As the new head politician, why not . . .

Make a political survey?

As the new top officer it would be in order to make a check on the company's financial status, business prospects, personnel available, and other such factors that might have something to do with your success. But how about the political situation in your company? A survey of this factor might be worth more to you than some of the checks you would do as a matter of course.

Explore all political groups

Each of the areas of politics that affect your job is concerned with people.

The people above you,

The people below you, and

The customers.

All can have a hand in making your job a success or failure. Take a sheet of typewriter paper. Divide the long way into two parts. Write at the top of these sections: above—below. Now under each make notes on the politics you have in each area.

Here are some thoughts on the left column of that chart— the power.

Keep the power on your side

You'll plan to do this, of course, but who is the power? One company president, whose boss had been moved upstairs to chairman, said, "They tell me that I'm the top executive officer, but I'll never be that as long as that guy's around." A second said, "They kicked the former president up to vice-chairman and I'm sure he is doing nothing to help me." What is your situation with such gentlemen?

The chairman or vice-chairman

What do you do about these gentlemen if you have been told you are the top executive officer and the man still stays on and tries to run the show or just nibs in? If you grew up as the assistant to the man, you know how to handle him. If you came in from the outside, you may have to check to find out how much power he has. He might assume he has it when he doesn't. One president advised, "Do something important without consulting him and you'll find out." That might be living dangerously, but it should produce results. Most executives I talked to suggest consulting the man even though you know his new title is a face-saving device. Others ask them to take assignments. "Try not to hurt his feelings," advised one president. "But there may be times when you have to have a showdown." Bear in mind that most of these ex-top executives have friends throughout the company, on the board, in the industry, and they can help you if they are willing to help. Your first approach to the power would be to find out how much power they retain, and appraise how much that power can be used to help or stymie you. Don't antagonize these men if you can avoid it.

The others to be cultivated

These vary with every company, but these could be——
a. Influential members of the board of directors
b. Key individual stockholders and stockholding groups
c. Important figures in industry, government
d. Customers

Whom do you have to please?

Maybe you're a rough, tough executive that hates the idea of catering to anybody, but now things have changed. Ask yourself, "Which members of the board of directors do I have to please?" and "Are there any important stockholders I should cultivate?" Then, "Is there anybody else?" Make a list of these people. Talk over this list with your friends on the board, the ones who were for you for this job. Work up a plan of cultivating these names so that they are with you on what you plan to do, and know how fine a job you're doing. This may mean luncheons, notes, telephone calls, the approach will probably vary with each man. With a little thought you can work out plans for a number of such contacts that don't take too much of your time. One executive said, "You have to eat lunch anyway." Talk to top executives in other companies and ask for suggestions on how they handle this type of contact. The politician in congress keeps his fences mended back home. Follow his example and do what you can to keep your name up with the people who can vote you out. Here are some thoughts to consider.

Members of the board of directors

Let's assume that one member of the board was positively against you. His reason may be as silly as, "He looks like my brother-in-law and my brother-in-law is no good." Such a character will be reluctant to admit he is wrong. What do you do about him? Or do you do anything? When you were interviewed for the job, the questions asked could indicate what doubts the committee had about you.

One president said, "Before I took over this job I was the president of a small company. Now I'm president of this large company. I know that the members of the board that selected me are watching me and asking themselves, 'Has his experience with the smaller company given him the know-how he needs to handle this larger job?' I've got to keep on selling those people, one eye on the job, the other on the audience. And that's politics, isn't it?" Because he knew the doubts of those above, he could work to allay those doubts.

The one eye on the job keeps the job going so that it meets with the approval of those above, and the other eye on the power keeps those above informed of the good job being done. Of course, not all of the members of the board have to have the full treatment. Some members may be there for window dressing. But determine which ones have to be sold and keep selling them.

Important stockholders

I attended the meeting of the stockholders of a large company and was talking to the president when a Mr. Curtis came by. The president greeted him as a long-time friend, and the chairman came over and escorted Mr. Curtis to a seat up front. "Who's Mr. Curtis?" I asked. "He's our next to largest stockholder," the president said. It may not be the largest stockholders that have the ear of the board. But a friendship with key individual stockholders may bring them to you with suggestions or complaints instead of to the board and it may keep them on the right side in proxy fights.

Watch the grandstand

A change in power relationships can clobber you. Here is one instance. I was hired to work as a consultant for one company by the president and the vice-president. At the time they were the power. The death of a large stockholder, the sponsor of my two friends, changed the picture. In a few months my friends were out and a new president and vice-president were in. The new management continued to work with me. I admit I never knew whether or not they went along with me to find out what the others had been planning. But they went along planning for the identical objectives of the first two. There was nothing wrong with the first two men. They were planning for the good of the company, but the change in power eased them out. Perhaps these men could not have helped themselves in this situation, the move came too suddenly. But the story shows why all power above should be considered.

Important figures. A president who goes on fishing trips with other presidents of companies shows evidence of personal power. Others that help this image are political party leaders, senators and congressmen, bankers, entrepreneurs, big operators. We laugh at name-dropping, but the dropping is to build an image. Are you in on any of this? If not, how can you get in?

Men in your industry. Members of the board and stockholders are impressed when these leaders in the industry seem to know and accept you as one of them. What can you do to build up your image with this group?

Call on the customers

In any company the most important power is the customers. Why not call on them? Supposing a member of the board meets one of the executives of a customer at his club or at a convention. The latter says, "That's a good man you got running the Ajax for you." That's a plus, isn't it? Then too it might help get business. One president told me, "We're growing faster than our two main competitors."

I asked, "Why do you think that is?"

"The sales department tells me it's because I call on the customers," he laughed.

"Don't the top executives of the competitors do that?" I asked.

"No, one was a lawyer and the other was an engineer. I suppose it is natural for them to stay away from the customers. I hope they don't start calling."

The top executive officer of a company should be its best salesman. He can get in to see the top men in his customer's organization, men the sales representative can't see, or might hesitate to try to see. He can talk plans on a higher level. He will hear things that will help him run his own job better.

If you call on the top man in the customer's place, the word goes down through the chain of command, "They got a progressive president over at Ajax, impressed the boss a lot." One top executive said, "I'm not too fond of making these calls, but I find myself doing more and more of it every year."

Selling and alibiing

One top executive said, "On this job a man has to do a lot of selling and alibiing." The selling applied to that news about the company that would interest the power above and the alibiing to those conditions over which the top executive has no control, such as economic changes, market changes, union relationships. You may have little control over these irritants, and some drop into your lap without notice. It is well to let the power know that you had nothing to do with these troubles. Here are some thoughts given me by top executives on how they handle them:

Economic changes. Business falls off, people stop buying. You do all you can to hold position, but nothing works. One vice-president, whose company was in a sales slump, said, "I wish business would pick up just a little bit." Just that little bit may be all that stands between you and unemployment compensation. In this case business didn't pick up and the V.P. was fired. Within ninety days after his successor was appointed, business picked up and the new man was a hero, at least for the duration of the boom.

Such economic changes may be a problem in the future. If they come, what do you plan to do? It's well to have your plan worked out.

Market changes. These can cause trouble through no fault of yours and can be due to factors that go back to before your time. Perhaps the former management decided not to change its product design. But the unpredictable public went overboard for the new design of your competitor. The company loses position, and you are asked, "What's happening?" You're on the spot through no fault of yours. But you are on it. What political moves should you plan when you see these changes coming so that in the minds of those that count the blame is associated with your predecessor? Perhaps you need some politics in a situation such as this. Surely you need more than the hopeful wish that the V.P. expressed to me.

Union relationships. Some members of the board may go for a policy of, "Give them nothing." You may agree, but you know this will not work. And so you have to be the artful dodger, go along with what the board wants, and yet have no great union trouble either. A strike, even an unauthorized sitdown, can change your image fast. You have one plus on this union question. Most members of the board are inclined to feel that all union leaders are illegitimate. Many of them will add depreciating adjectives. Thus any explanations will be accepted more readily.

What were you hired to do?

In selling the power you are trying to show them that you are doing the job they hired you to do better than anyone else can do it. Thus it pays to have that job clearly in mind. Let's say you present a fine image to the public. That's an asset, of course, but did the power hire you to present a fine image to the public? What did they hire you to do? The following describes the respective company board's assignments to four top executive officers of companies:

Number One was brought in from outside to clean out the

deadwood. "My assignment is to be ruthless about this. Fire the inefficient, forget years of service. Make the best separation deals that I can. Put younger men on their jobs." This job is a stinker, one that called for a tough operator, but the man knew exactly what he was assigned to do.

"What happens when you get this streamlining done?" I asked.

"Then I go too. I'm not kidding myself. SOBs have to move on."

Number Two was brought in from the outside to get the company off dead center and moving. It hadn't been keeping up with its industry.

"I've built up two other companies, and they think I can build this one," he said. His problem was laid out for him. The power had told him clearly what he was to do.

Number Three was put on the job because the top executive officer had passed away. "They wanted to keep the company running just as it was. So my assignment was to keep moving and not rock the boat." That man also had a clear assignment.

Number Four was brought in to get the company in the black. "They told me, 'No matter how you do it, get it done.' That's clear, isn't it? But I know that as I start to clear up some of these bottlenecks, there will be screaming, and the board will be asking why I did it this way." His assignment was clear to him, but he saw that he might have to do a bit of selling to get permission to do what was needed.

What is your assignment?

Your position may not be parallel to any of these four. But do you have a clear assignment? Do you know what you can do? Can you do what you want to do instead of doing what someone else wants you to do? Are you the boss or a figure-head? In the old days, when the top man owned the business, his word was law. He said, "Scram," and everybody scrammed. But mighty few professional managers are in that position. The latter had better ask, "Can I use my power to get things done?"

Write down on paper a one-page description of what you think your assignment is. Then talk this over with the power. Get their agreement that this is it.

You're in the same position as the baseball manager

You are much like the manager of a baseball team. Anything can get you fired. And that same anything can make you a hero. If things go OK, you are OK. If things go wrong, you might go with them. The baseball manager has to have the fans on his side. As the top executive of a company, you need a larger group of allies. Particularly you need the power above on your side.

I talked to an executive who was given a top job in a company that had distribution centers all over the country. His job was to get the centers operating more efficiently. He moved in on the job, fired all but the efficient managers of the centers. Then he got the ax. "I was only doing what I thought they wanted me to do," he complained. He didn't understand his assignment. Management wanted the centers run efficiently, but they didn't want morale shot to pieces.

Use practical techniques

Chapter 10 gave you a number of suggestions on how to work with the boss politically. Many of these can be used with the men above you who can affect your tenure. Now instead of one boss to please, you probably have a number of bosses. Each of these is different in what he thinks you should be. Your first step is to find out what each wants. Then in your contacts with him show him you are doing what he wants. Here are ways mentioned:

Keep contact. Perhaps you can do this with a telephone call or a luncheon now and then or a dinner. If not, do it by mail. Perhaps the company sends him the house organ. You might take over this job in his case, send him the magazine with a note referring to something in the magazine that might interest him. A scribbled note on the cover can make his copy more personal.

Build your image. If you agree to talk to the investment counselors, you might let him know of the invitation, ask his suggestions on what to say, or have him check a part of your speech. You might get him a seat at the head table. Make a good talk and you help build his approval. Chapter 21 gives a number of suggestions for image building.

Make him a part of your public relations. If you have to send out a newspaper release on some phase of the company's business, send it to him, perhaps with that scribbled note. He may miss the story in the newspaper. The newspaper story may be for the general public but these few important men above you are your public. Work out ways to give them a little better treatment than you would the masses.

Dramatize yourself. Plan any dramatization of yourself to line up with the assignment you have. Most jobs would call for the top man to show drive, punch, get up and go, but maybe your assignment was to keep the ship going ahead without rocking the boat. And that might call for the strong, silent man. It might be helpful to develop your speaking talents to the point where you are the best public speaker in the industry, in demand everywhere. Your public relations man may want to put you on the speaking circuit, but analyze this thoroughly. Is this what the power wants?

Keep informed. When a new product is developed, one company president sends the circular to each of the men above with a short note. "My powerful ten like this attention," he states. If the union paper prints something favorable to the company, get copies and send that out. Broadcast any information that shows you are doing the job assigned to you.

Anticipate bad news. The economists say that conditions will not be too favorable. Let these top men know how this might affect the earning picture for this quarter. If a top executive quits, get together the reasons and let your superiors know why. Do this even if you engineered the separation. If a competitor pulls a coup, get together the reasons why you didn't think of it first. This is a part of the alibiing that helps you keep your job.

Educate on the business. Perhaps some of these important men are on the board because their names add prestige to the list. If they know little about the business, it might be worthwhile to help them understand why your company does things one way, while in their businesses it is done another way.

One more thought——

Be honest with yourself

You can be replaced. Remember you're expendable. If you want to hold this top job, try to make your demise a tough decision. Keep in mind those questions that the board is asking as they think of firing you. Can we get a better man? Is it better to take a chance on a newcomer than to go along with this fellow? If we fire this man now after such a short tenure, will it be easy to get a good man to replace him? You know the power will be asking such questions. Play your hand so that there will be real doubt as to whether or not a new man would be as good as you are.

Don't overdo. Any of these suggestions may well go with some of your power and not go so well with others. Figure out which will be helpful in your situation and which will not. I asked a member of the board of directors of a company why the company president had resigned. "The guy was always trying to sell us," he said. It is possible to sell too hard.

Accept the facts of life

Most of the advice in this chapter could be summed up in this sentence, "Organize your job so that you have time to do what is needed to run the job and still have time to handle the political assignments with those above you. Think of these basic steps:

1. Get your assignment straight. What exactly does the power want you to do?

2. Make a list of the men who have the power to keep you on this job or throw you off it.

3. Plan and carry out your selling and alibiing to keep these men on your side.

4. Don't forget the customers. Top executives seldom get fired when business is good.

Now about that politics below you.

17

Survey the Politics below

These people all work for you. And some of them work for themselves too. Some of that work for themselves is for the good of the company, some of it is in the interest of the employee alone. In working up the chart on the politics in your company, I'm sure that you have thought of such things as—feuding—cliques—social life—friendships—departments —bureaucrats—powerful subordinates—family—church or fraternal affiliation—recreation. Perhaps in your situation only a few of these apply.

If you came up from the ranks you probably have a good idea of the internal political situation that now faces you. But, if you came in from the outside, you have to find out what goes. One president stated, "I was brought in from the outside and after I got in I found two men who were capable of handling this job, both able, both efficient, both doing a good job for the company. I want to keep them doing that good job, don't I?"

Another top man told me of sit-downers, the entrenched department heads who had been having their way for years and could see no reason why he should change their setup. Another said, "Why, even my secretary, the one they assigned to me, resented me. And she let me know it in a lot of ways."

Some of these situations you discover rather quickly, but others you have to dig out.

What it means to you

I've said that company politics can kill you dead. It can. One executive told me, "I'll stamp on it at every opportunity, in time it will be all gone." But it won't go away. You can curb it. You can keep it within reasonable bounds. You can turn it to the advantage of the company. You can put it to work for you. But stop it, you can't.

Here are ten reasons why you have to know about it.

1. Executives may leave for other jobs because they can't take the politicking.

2. Your company gets a reputation as a political hot bed and you will not be able to hire the outside executives you want.

3. Promising young men on the way up leave to get away from it.

4. Promotions may not go to the most competent.

5. Decisions may be held up.

6. The firm may be held back because certain of the intrenched will not allow needed changes.

7. Sit-downs may hold up projects.

8. Costs may go up because a change to a more efficient operation may eliminate certain jobs.

9. Decisions may be made on the basis of benefit they give an individual or department rather than company.

10. Endless bickering may delay decisions.

These are but a few of the losses to you and your firm that were mentioned by executives I interviewed, and each told me about specific instances where these things had happened in his firm. I asked, "Why does your top management allow this?" The reason I got most often was, "I wonder if they know it?"

I suggest you know about the various types of politicking in your firm, and know who the politickers are. By knowing the different types and the executives playing each type, you can do what you can to keep the politics within manageable limits.

The good guys and the bad guys

You're not too much concerned with the fellow who sits on the rock and directs the pursuers with, "They went thata way." You want the fellows riding the horses. Some are good, some bad. And even the good may need some curbing.

If you feel all politics is bad, then all politics is bad for your company. If you feel some of it is helpful, then what phases are helpful? This is your decision to make. Here are some questions to ask about politics as you look over your chart:

Ask yourself these questions:

a. What types of politics are being played in my company?
b. Who is responsible for each type?

c. What types hurt the company?

d. Which types help us, or do us no harm?

e. What can I do to keep politics within reasonable limits?

f. How can I channel the activities of the politicians to do the company the most good?

g. Am I or is my office responsible for any of it?

All these questions indicate why you can't turn your back on company politics.

How to flush out the politics

These suggestions, given by executives, might help you check on politics.

Praise or criticism. If you hear criticism of a man or department from a number of sources, check it through. A group may be ganging up on somebody. Analyze why three men should criticize Chauncey, who are the three, what is their tie in with each other, what can they gain out of it? If certain men bring you information on what's wrong with a part of the operation, never what's right, check why? One executive said, "When I get this kind of criticism, I ask the bearer, 'What's right with this operation?' Usually his answer shows me that he is unprepared on this side of the question. But on the wrong side, he's loaded."

The same thing goes for praise. Is there a job in prospect that this man getting all the kudos might fill? What you hear may be on the level. If it is you may want to do something about it, but check.

Then why should the three be boosting Angus for the job? Is he a relative or something?

Analyze each bit of praise or criticism to see what's behind it.

How about powerful subordinates?

These men may be after your job. You can't blame them for that. And perhaps this competition is good politics. They may be valuable to the company and you want to retain them. One executive told me, "I control this piece of business and it amounts to about 20 per cent of the entire company business." A man controlling that much business might feel that he is more important than he is, not expendable, or that he is unappreciated. Another executive told me, "I'm on a first-name basis with every member of the board." Such men may be valuable to you or dangerous. Why not work out projects for them that build their stature and also builds yours. The men with power will surely do something. Why not direct what they do toward your objectives.

Does it take too long to get decisions? Delay may indicate that some clique is figuring out how to come up with the answer so that none of their group gets hurt. It may be that the group has learned that if they stall long enough this danger will go away. One president said, "I came in from the outside, and the bureaucrats figured they could slow me up. When I asked for a report on a minor phase of the business, they told me it would take six days. And it would have taken six days if I didn't move in." Another said, "If a decision is up to one man it may be that he is trying to get as many in on it as possible, trying to spread the responsibility so that if something goes wrong it wasn't his decision alone." A second put in, "Then too his delay may be due in part to the fact that the others want no part of the decision." A third executive said, "I had this when I first came on this job. But I got the habit of asking for a decision by a certain date. 'I'll need the answer Thursday,' I said. The dead line got me the answers, screams too. But maybe I didn't do anything but make the politickers work faster."

Any delay gives the politicians time to get in their work. It gives time for rumors to spread. One top man told me about two of his subordinates taking the news of a change he proposed to one of the prominent stockholders. In a short time he had a number of the higher-ups asking him why he wanted to make such a change. He had asked for a report and he was into intrigue up to his neck. Check any such delay. You asked Pete to do this job. Why hasn't he moved in on it?

How hot is the rumor mill? Perhaps not too many of the rumors will get into your office, but ask those below you, "What good rumors have you heard lately?" You'll probably have to break through the palace guard to reach the right people for this answer. But figure out how you can get through this iron curtain. When the vice-president offers to drive you to the airport, turn him down. Tell him, "The company can't afford to pay that much for a chauffeur." Let one of the assistants do it. Then don't sleep on the way, talk to the driver.

If the rumor mill is active, what inspires the rumors? Rumors may sound amusing and they may be ridiculous, but they can hurt you. One designing group started a rumor that the company in the Middle West was going to move the factory down into the South. The factory payroll was important to the small town and all hell broke loose. Before the rhubarb was settled, a new management took over. The old management hadn't planned to move. A southern community had contacted them with a proposal. And that was enough for the group that wanted the top man's head. Rumors can hurt morale. Check the rumors, try to analyze why each was started. If the mill is active, it is an indication that the politicians are at work.

Buck-passing. With the clear lines of authority set up you can't have too much of this, but if you have any of it, check to see why. Are the two department heads feuding? Is one out to get the other? Is the apparent confusion due to a fear of making mistakes? You'll probably get this buck-passing with the type of politician not struggling for power but trying to avoid responsibility. Perhaps the department head is one who says, "Let the other fellow make the mistakes." And in the meantime nothing happens. He doesn't move because the last guy that moved is no longer with us. You may have to redefine the authority each executive has, and make certain that each understands his responsibility.

Usurping authority. Usually the department head who is trying to take over from another does not come to you and say, "Jerry isn't doing a job on this. Here's how he should be doing it." He moves in in subtle ways. He may show you how he can handle a part of the work with less cost. If he took over, the company could lay off three or four of the men in the other department. Such attempts cause confusion. One fellow fighting to grab, another fighting to keep. You have to listen to a lot of guff from both sides that would not be necessary if the two would stick to the job assigned them. The executives who are being undermined lose confidence in you. Move in on any indication of this type of politics fast. It may be that the work should be moved as the intriguer suggests. If so, move it, but don't let the confusion drag on.

Diagram the cliques. Who runs with whom? Which fellows have lunch together, which make up the golf foursome? These men may be competing with each other for your job, but they are a gang with a certain amount of power and they want to keep that power. Are there opposing cliques? Let's say one member of a clique brings a proposal to you. You ask, "Do you think the other executives will aprove this?" Back he comes with the word of the approval of the boys in this golf foursome of his. This may be the right group and then again other opinions should be had. If so, ask him to check the proposal with others.

Check members of your clique. Analyze the members of your team. Why are they on it? Check each man. Is Jim there because he has strong needs of security and needs support from above to make him feel secure? Is Tick on because you have defined his job responsibilities in such a way that his own security is dependent on his cooperation with you? Is Pete on because you like the way he never worries about anything? Did you take Jock in because of the laughs he brings? Abe because he yesses you? Then what politics do these men generate because they are close to you? How much help is each member of this group to you?

Survey the turnover of executives. A turnover of executives can indicate that politics is afoot. This applies to top executives and to the young men coming up. Executives may leave because they have to spend too much time fighting the politicians or they have to politick to hold on, or they don't want to politick. Young men may leave because they see what the politicians do to stymie projects or the progress of men the youngsters think able. If your company has an exit interview that attempts to find out why these men leave, get yourself a spot in this exit interview. If you have no such plan, do the exit interview yourself. Talk plainly to these men.

Ask them, "Would you mind telling me the real reason why you are leaving?" Some will give you the real reason. You might ask, "Did you find that company politics helped or hindered you in your work here?" If politics is his reason, he may come clean and tell you what is going on and what you should do about it.

Does it show in department reports? Check the department reports carefully for any criticism of other departments. Reread such lines as, "We are unable to tell the effect of this move because of inadequate information from the accounting department," or "This survey was started by the marketing department but was not completed according to our best information." Check to see what's going in such cases. Is somebody trying to sabotage another department? The statement may mean nothing, but then again, it may be a part of the political line.

How about conflicts? It may seem obvious that wherever there is continued conflict there is politics, between men or departments. As in party politics, you'll always have the liberals and the conservatives, the one faction for change, the second for the *status quo*. If there is a dispute on policy, check to see what is back of it. It may be an honest disagreement, and then it might come because the good idea was Hank's and someone doesn't want to see Hank get the credit. Usually a few questions can determine the worth of any such disagreement on policy. If the man honestly disagrees, he will be able to answer your questions with good reasons why.

Line up the competitors. You can probably put your finger on the source of much of the politics if you make a study of who is competing with whom. Such competition is healthy if it is channeled correctly. Two men competing with each other for a job ahead are more inclined to give their present jobs all they have. Encourage this competition. A man is not worth the better job without a competitive spirit. Keep this competition working for the company. Move in on it at the first indication that somebody is pulling a knife.

Check Mr. Big. Are you generating any politics? One top executive told me, "I had a habit of bringing the top two men into my office every morning and we'd spend about one hour discussing the business. I didn't see anything wrong with that until I found out that the help was calling this group 'the management team.'" Let's say you were a company politician. When someone asked, "What are the big shots discussing this A.M.?" would you be without an idea? And so a rumor is started. Another president said, "I used this Charley to run errands for me and the people around the place got to think of us as buddy buddies. I didn't know it, but it seems Charlie wasn't doing a lick of work on his regular job. When I caught up with that, I asked, 'Why don't you fire him?' His manager said, 'I didn't think I could. He was such a pal of yours.'" Top men generate this type of politics without knowing they are doing it. One man's secretary keeps the men she doesn't like out of the boss's office. And who do the executives think is responsible? An executive assistant to the big man asks for data in such a way that the executives resent it. They feel the boss asked him to get that tough. The top man attends the fraternal meeting. Is the fraternal group using him? Check through your operation and see if you are giving any false impressions. And if you are generating any of this politics, why shouldn't the boys down below feel that this is one of the qualifications of the big shot, so they do a bit of politicking, just to get their hand in, of course.

To sum up on politics below you

As you look over this politics below you, ask yourself what's good and what's bad. What's working for the company? What's harming it? Who are the big politickers? How many of them are spending more time politicking than working at the jobs for which they are paid? Ask yourself quite a few such questions but follow this advice and you can't go far wrong.

1. Don't say, "We haven't any." Remember that was the reply of Simple Simon to the Pieman.

2. Know what's cooking and put your finger on the cooks.

3. Accept responsibility for dealing with what politics you find. It's your job. You're on the spot about which President Harry Truman said, "The buck stops here."

4. Try to stamp out the politics that's hurting the company or you.

Now some thoughts on how to deal with politics and the politickers.

18

Keep Company Politics from Getting You

What do you want this company politics to do—continue the march—drop dead? You can help it do either. But most of all you want it to help the company and to help you. How do you do that? If you were trying to answer that question, you would probably go to executives who had had some experience in shaping company politics to the benefit of their companies. I did just that, and this chapter will pass on the suggestions these men gave me.

Many of these suggestions are good common sense, some may seem a bit Machiavellian, but all help you hold onto that top job of yours. Some sound like good human relations, the type of thing that rates you as a good boss, but what's wrong with that? Why not check to see how you rate on these suggestions? And, if you rate low, plan what you can do to better your rating.

Enjoy success

This does not mean that it will help to start having three cocktails before dinner instead of the usual two. Celebrate, yes, hold a celebration, sing the victory song, but don't drag it out. Celebrate too long and you become bored with success, take it for granted. And that attitude can kill you. That first victory came hard, the second may be more difficult, the ones after that may call for more drive, ingenuity, effort. As you celebrate victory one, prepare for victory two. Keep something ahead that is bigger and better, something that will give you a greater feeling of accomplishment. As the top man, you have a continuing reason for work and accomplishment. You've won once, now how do you keep on winning? How can you build on what has been done? How can you go ahead? How can you use this victory as a stepping stone to the next? To paraphrase Satchel Page, "While you're celebratin', somebody may be gaining on you." Enjoy your kick over this first victory, but, as you celebrate, think about what's next.

Keep from being isolated

You have that nice office with the fine furniture and you can go into it and go to sleep, practice putting on that thick rug, or do whatever you want. You can get yourself a secretary that keeps just about everybody out. But that won't help you hold the job. Reverse this process, go out and meet the people. One factory manager brought in from outside to run a plant went out into his new factory and worked on the production line for three weeks. Some executives would call that grandstanding. But he learned more about the factory and how it was run in that short time than he could have found out in months from his assistants or from factory trips. He talked to workers' union stewards, straw bosses, department managers. He was better-informed than if he talked to his assistants, wasn't he? One company general manager took a two-hour ride to the airport with a young executive from the factory as chauffeur. As they left the factory, the top man said, "I had a hard night last night and I'm going to sleep on this trip." The executive needed the sleep more than the information he might get, didn't he? I asked the man who told me this, "Does that fellow seem to be on top of what is going on?" His answer was, "Ed, we never can tell about him."

When I was checking about how different top men keep in touch, one executive said, "My boss has a good one. He asks, 'You don't have any secrets I should know, do you?' Lays himself wide open, doesn't he?"

Here is a suggestion—if you feel that communication up to your office is not as good as it should be, make a list of ways you can check on what's going on. Not more reports, for the reports the boys send you might be slanted at making things look better than they are. Meetings, visits, factory tours—such things as that.

The best way to keep on top of your job is to be alert for information and opportunities to pick it up. Of course, you have to check each item but in the checking you learn more about what is going on. Get out of the ivory tower—get down to the people.

Keep your executives from being isolated

Some good executives find it difficult to get close to the people under them. Try to make setups so that the executives see the workers often. One check to make is the location of the supervisors' offices. Are they close to the workers they supervise? This seems simple, but check also the executive's habits. Does he go into the office in the morning, close his door, and make any visitor feel unwelcome? You can excuse such methods by saying, "Amos is a character, that's his way of operating." Get Amos out of his shell, meeting the people, finding out what is going on. Some executives may get in the hair of their subordinates too much. Others not enough. But which is better for the job the man holds? The other day an executive said, "Nothing happens in that guy's factory that he doesn't know about in ten minutes." That manager isn't isolated, is he? One of the jobs of the top man is to teach his subordinates to work with people. Suggest getting the answers to questions such as, "What are your workers complaining about?" Most supervisors will report, "Nothing that I know of." OK, send him out to find out. Have him bring his findings to you. Suggest monthly meetings of his staff. Assign jobs such as bringing information to his group. Ask him to tell you how they took it. The executive who likes isolation will stay isolated if you don't nudge him a bit.

Explain most important decisions

When you make an important decision, perhaps a change in policy, explain it to the higher executives. Make sure they understand well enough to explain it to the top men in their commands. This explanation to the help shows them that it is important to get behind the decision and sell it to their employees. I helped the president of a company make up a chart presentation that he planned to give to his associates explaining a change in distribution. I'm sure that the trouble he went to in making up those charts helped convince the help that his decision was made after a detailed study. One of his assistants asked him, "Can I have those charts to help me explain this to my people?"

On most important decisions you may want the advice of your assistants. And these men may divide into two groups, one for certain action, the other against it. You can't go along with both groups. In such cases it is well to let the group that lost out know why you decided as you did. Talk to or telephone the men in this group and explain. A letter or memo might not do the job properly, but a two-way conversation has a better chance. Explain that the againsters' views were considered, his points made sense, but———. If the decision does not work out well, your explanation will cut down such expressions as, "Well, I advised him what to do, but he wouldn't listen to me."

This, of course, applies to promotions. The man who didn't get the job wonders why he wasn't chosen. Let him know that he was or was not considered. If these reasons mean that he is not promotable, tell him that too. If his shortcomings are ones that he can correct, he may want to work on them.

Your setup may be such that you can say, "This is it, like it or else. . . ." But it helps morale to explain. If you don't explain, someone else will dream up an explanation.

When you have an important decision to make, work up a list of all who should be advised. You want both your bosses and your help with you on it. Getting everybody in on this explanation is good politics. The boys spend their time explaining instead of wondering why.

Keep all hands informed, but . . .

Decide who should be informed and about what. Ask what they know, what they should know. Management agrees that, if the group knows what the shooting is for, it will do better shooting. Because workers are informed, they feel that they are in on things so they feel more important. Psychologists tell you this. But hold it. There is some information that should not be given out at all. One local company was in danger of losing certain business that accounted for about one-fourth of the production of the plant. If the business was lost, there would be a large cut in the employment of the factory. Somehow the information leaked, and the newspaper printed a story, "It is rumored that this may happen, but the management will not confirm or deny." Reading this iffy story workers in the factory became concerned, so did the chamber of commerce and the local merchants. The management knew that information such as this should not be released until there was no chance of holding the business.

One of the human-relations rules is, "Keep the workers informed." But don't go overboard on this. This advice applies to news of the future of the company, plans for expansion, acquisitions, moving of factories, giving up a certain line, mergers, or other company moves that affect the well-being of the workers. You may have some future plans that mean much to the workers and you want to put a press release on them, but how much do you want to give out? Your publicity man may want to shoot the works for his record is his scrap book of newspaper clippings. But check any news for timing and for how much to release. Make a setup so that you see each news release or general letter to the help before it is sent out. Experience may have shown you that a certain type of news is bound to leak out. You'll have to release this. One president advised, "Check release of information with the question, 'Will this help or harm the company?'" I once edited a company magazine and telephoned a vice-president to check on some information I got through the grapevine. "I don't know," he said. "They never tell me anything." What should I think of a V.P. who spoke of the power as "they"? If you keep the employees informed, they are more inclined to think of the company as "We." Some information should go down the line all the way, some only so far, some should stay in the front office. Decide which and try to keep it the way you decide.

Check the flow of information

What gets through, how much, is the information understood? Perhaps you have relied on letters to department heads and the setup is for them to pass on the information. Some executives don't trust letters. They say it is better to telephone the man and tell him. Telephone contact is personal—man to man. On the phone you can ask if you are making yourself clear. One executive told me of a check he made to see how much information got through. He used his usual system, a letter to his four department heads. Later he checked the thirty-two men who should have had the information. "I was amazed," he reported, "how little these men had absorbed." He now is using personal contact or the telephone, and he suggests that all of his department heads do the same.

Executives tell me, "We need training on communication around here." This is true in most companies. But the boss is likely to think that the faulty communication is in other departments, not in his office. At a management conference the other day, I saw a speaker pass out a paragraph for a group to read. Then he asked each man to tell him what the paragraph meant. His demonstration showed how letters can be misinterpreted and misunderstood. Each of the thirteen men read the same words, but the interpretations varied enough to help the speaker make his point. And all of the words were simple words. I'd suggest you check your communication from the top down. Work up a simple plan that tells you whether or not you are getting important information through to the people who should have it. When you rough out a letter·to send out, ask three people to read it and tell you what it means. Their reports on what you said may help you make the meaning clearer.

Check employee worries about the company

In a recent article in a management magazine the following reasons were given for executive worries about the future of their companies: the future of the industry, of the company in the industry, fear of merger, of acquisition by a competitor, inroads of competition, unprogressive management, too much family. Survey the situation of your company and ask, "Should any of our men worry about any of these things?" If they should, talk frankly about any of these fears. You know more than the executive does, and in so many cases his worries are based on nothing.

Give responsibility to individuals, not committees

A committee operation might seem like a team operation at the start, but remember Boss Kettering's quote when his wife told him that Lindbergh had made his historic flight to Paris. He said, "A committee would never have made it." Just consider the mechanics of a committee. First, you have to get the members together. That means delay. Then everybody has to have his say. More delay. Then three gang up on two and that means politics. The one-man decision can come faster, the individual can hold his meeting anytime, he needs no help in thinking out the subject. And so you get a decision, one that he thought out and likes. There is no compromise. The individual knows every angle and has his reasons for it. No phase need be explained by, "Well, I wasn't too much for that part, but Hondo was a member of the committee and we had to let him have his way on something." Give the job to men, not groups.

Build your assistants

Today you hear much talk that tells you, "All development is self-development." But the boss can help along this development. The other day, a clerk in an office showed me a plan his boss had suggested for reminding himself of the jobs he had to do that day. It was a simple memo pad on which at the start of each morning he wrote down the jobs he had to do that day, and as he did one he crossed it off. When a new one came up he added it to the list. The next day he started with the jobs he hadn't done yesterday and added the ones for the new day that he knew about. "It's a good idea, isn't it?" the young man asked. It was a good idea and a demonstration of how the boss helps the assistant learn. This applies also to helping your top assistants. First know what each needs, then help him get what he needs. The man under you learns if you give him challenging assignments, work he has never done before. I once was asked to call on a dozen of the top stockholders of my company and explain an executive compensation plan that was to be voted on. I told my boss, "I have never done anything like this before." He said, "I know that. I want you to learn to do this type of thing." An executive does this when he asks his employee, "How would you suggest doing this job?" Or when he allows the man to do the job his way. Recently I read an article in which the associates of Robert S. McNamara, Secretary of Defense, claimed that the secret of his management of the Department of Defense was the simple word "Why." It will pay any executive to learn this technique. A subordinate wants to start a project. You ask why. If he gives you a good answer, you know that he has thought about his plan. If he can't give you a good answer, he learns not to approach you without a good answer to your "why." You build men by teaching them such techniques. McNamara gives written questions and asks for written answers. A written answer has to be thought out. Let's say you put a new man on a job. You hand him a long list of questions about the job. You say, "Why don't you get the answers to these questions and in about two weeks we'll talk about them?" He'd learn that job faster than he would without the questions, wouldn't he? Think of these management devices that you might use to develop your men. Too many of them will stand still if you don't encourage them.

Let your employees know they can make mistakes

The fallacy of the SOB-type of management is that it has everybody running so scared that nobody will take a chance on making a mistake. When a man feels that, if he makes a mistake, he is out, he will spend his time trying to keep from making mistakes, not in trying to improve the work of his department. Let the man know that you want him to make decisions. Explain that he will make mistakes. You expect that. If he is right a certain percentage of the time, he is doing as well as management generally. I've seen figures that say if a manager is right in 58 per cent of his decisions, he is doing fine. That leaves a lot of margin for error, doesn't it? Don't expect all of your men to be up to your standards. They shouldn't be, you're the top man. Try to train them to come up to your standards, but don't rail at them if they can't make it. Admit your mistakes, you've been wrong at times and will be again. Use the "I made a mistake like that once" technique to help a man over a bad time after he has pulled a boo-boo. Men will make mistakes if they make decisions. Recognize this and encourage the decision making even though you know the mistakes will come.

Recognize work well done

I rode up in the elevator from the fourth floor to the ninth with a company vice-president. He greeted one of the men in the elevator with, "Buck, that was a good job you did with the Parish Company." "Thanks," Buck said as he got off at the fifth floor. Even though there was no more conversation, Buck would tell the wife about that contact when he came home that night. It was probably the highlight of his day. For all the Bucks in your employ want to be respected as persons. They want the status symbols that are joked about— the title, the office, the name on the door, the company car, the club membership. They feel that these symbols are a re-

ward for work well done. One executive said, "If I do something wrong I hear about it fast, but when I do a good job,
nobody murmurs." It is OK to criticize. In most cases it helps
the man, but give him a pat on the back now and then too.

Reward talent

Let all know that talent is what counts around the company. Let them know that merit counts through money and
other types of compensation. Pass out the rewards equally and
fairly. Forget prejudices. You don't like the looks of a certain
man, he always needs a haircut. But he is producing more
work than some of the fellows who get a haircut every week.
Don't pass over Mr. Shaggy when you pass out the rewards.
Pay him for what he produces, even more than some of the
dandies that are up to your standard of dress. Check your
salary administration setup. Why do some get increases, others
no increases? You may find many deserving men that are not
being paid what they should be paid and what your salary
plan calls for. I once told the salary administration man of a
company I worked for about a certain man who had not had
a salary merit increase for two years. He said, "That can't
happen." Then he outlined the policy of the company on increases. If the managers adhered to that policy, no man doing
good work could go one year without a merit increase. But
the managers were not following the policy.

Each time a new union contract was signed, one company
passed on a percentage increase to the salary employees who
did not belong to the union. Who gave the workers these
increases? The union, wasn't it? And with that setup the managers could tell a man who asked for more money, "You just

got that 5 per cent last month." An executive wants merit increases. He wants some recognition that he is doing good for the company.

Check job and pay classifications

One executive said, "We make our workers unhappy by these job classifications we have. You can pay a man only what the classification calls for, from a low of this to a high of this. A fellow may be on the same job for ten years. Now he is getting the top pay for his classification. When he asks for a raise, his boss tells him, 'You're at the top of your classification.' This seems ridiculous, doesn't it? The man is doing a good job, but you can't boost his pay." Check to see if you have any such bottlenecks. If the worker is that good, work out some extra pay for tenure. Another mistake of these rating experts is that they rate a job on its repetitive nature. This may be a good basis for rating, but don't tell the man that his job is of a repetitive nature. He can think of many instances where he has to use his head and everyday at that.

Pay well enough

One of the executives I interviewed, a vice-president of a manufacturing company, told me of the large salary increase he had just received. The boost almost doubled what he was getting. "The boss wanted me to stay on this job so that I wouldn't think the only way I could do better was to get a promotion."

"Were you looking around?" I asked.

"No, but I had thought some of it—but a boost like this proves that I'm doing as well here as I could anywhere, doesn't it?"

Count the number of top positions in your company. There are only so many. Then make a head check of the number of men that might feel they could reach those top positions. You'll probably find more eligible men than positions. OK, then why not work out a pay scheme so that those valuable men earn enough so that they do not feel they are failures if they do not reach the top jobs.

Keep on top of morale

You read the results of surveys of employee opinion. 46 per cent take advantage of the coffee breaks, 54 per cent do not. Interesting, isn't it? At times it is possible to select some of the points of unrest developed by such surveys and do something about them. I'd suggest you make your checks on more practical matters. Here is a suggestion—a firm of career consultants—that may be a nicer name for a firm that is trying to lure one or more of your key men away from you—listed these causes of why men want to change jobs. These are given in the order of importance to the executives.

1. Unsatisfactory bosses
2. Limited advancement
3. Poor pay (note this is not first)
4. Lack of recognition
5. Unsatisfactory working conditions
6. Uncongenial associates
7. Security threatened

You can do something about every one of these seven reasons. But you can't do anything about it unless you know it exists. As you look over the list you may throw out some of these as not applying to your company at all. But are you sure? In my work with companies I have often been surprised at how little the top men knew about what was agitating the men down below. An executive down below says, "The company is too conservative." There is nothing wrong with being conservative. But the man's statement indicates that nobody has explained to him why the company does better by being conservative. And is the man with this thought likely to bring in an idea for improvement? A lack of morale doesn't show on the surface. You have to dig for it. So dig. It pays.

Keep your good men

Last week I asked a young executive why he had quit a job on which he was doing well. "I doubled my pay," he explained.

"That's great," I said, "but what was the second reason?" And that is a good question. In this case it brought out quite a few reasons that I doubt the top man in his company knew.

Most of us do not want to change, we resent change of any kind. And so, when the job pirate approaches your young executives, you have a strong force going for you. That fear of change. Another factor is that the executive knows you and is more inclined to take your word than that of the recruiter for he knows that no recruiter can be fully aware of what goes on inside the new company.

One executive told me of procedure he uses and that has helped him hold three out of four promising young men that had better job offers. He brought the men into his office and talked over the man's thinking on why he felt he had a better opportunity elsewhere. His interview was based on the following questions:

1. Do you feel that you have made a strong effort to work out a solution to your problems here?

2. On the new job are you getting at least a 25 per cent salary increase with equal pension benefits?

3. How much has your pay increased here in the past ten years?

4. Have you been passed over for promotion? How many times?

5. What have you done to prepare yourself for promotion?

6. Why do you feel you are on a blind-alley job here?

7. Do you feel you have been on one job too long?

8. Are you in a part of the business you don't like?

9. Are the personality conflicts that bother you too great to be worked out?

The purpose of the interview is to help the man analyze what the new job means to him and to compare it with his present job. You and he both have a good picture of his opportunities with your company. Neither of you know too much about the new job. You can, of course, bring up the names of other men that have left. Charlie left two years ago and he has had three jobs since. Emory left three years ago and he was out of a job for a long time. This may seem like dirty pool. But some pirate is trying to steal a good man from you, a man that you have spent time and money training, and that so-and-so pirate has done a dirty selling job, hasn't he? If you are squeamish, just mention the names of the men that left and didn't do so well. Let the man figure out how the rosy dreams of these others worked out. Don't allow good men to go over the hill without a fight. You may be doing them a favor to get them to stay.

Be frank with those who indicate a desire to get to the top

When the comer tells you that he wants your job, say, "That's great." Agree that he should want it. But, if all he has is a great desire, point out the other things he needs. Ask him, "What training do you think you need before you will be ready?" Then, "What are you doing about this training now?" An employment interview uses the question, "What is your ambition?" The counseling interview asks, "What job do you want within the company?"

By talking to the man frankly about his ambitions you let him know that you are aware of his interest in advancement. You can tell him that you are not opposed to the idea or that you are opposed to the idea and in the latter case you can tell him why. If your reasons are based on deficiencies he can correct, he can work to prepare himself. In all cases, let him know that he does not have to build himself a political machine to help him move onto your job. One president told an aspiring manager, "Bill, your background has been largely in purchasing. What do you think would be the best way in the company to get the training you need in other phases of the company's business?" Bill suggested a job rotation plan and the company is now trying it.

Some of the good men in the company don't want the top jobs. But when one says he does, even, "I want your job," tell him you are glad to hear that and point out how he can equip himself for it. Perhaps not by trying to sell you on his qualifications but by doing a good job where he is.

Put the politicians to work for company growth

You can't stop politics, no matter how good your intentions, so why not put the politickers to work building the company? Get them so interested in future projects that they have no time to play politics for the jobs ahead. Let's consider three fields in which most companies can grow. Technology, competition, diversification. OK, give your ambitious subordinate a job that would make him an expert in one of these fields or in others that better fit your business. Assign one man to study technology—this is such a broad subject that perhaps two or three men could be put on different phases of it. Competition—plenty of work can be done here, even though your company is a leader in your industry now. Diversification—have one man to check the possibility of adding this line, another this one. The men who take over these assignments are challenged by the project. They feel they are accomplishing something as they gather the data. If a man's report is negative, he feels he has saved the company from making a mistake. But the big advantage of this plan is that the executive is working for the growth of the company rather than for his own interests. Of course, such activities do create new businesses that might create new executive jobs, and this gives the politickers more jobs to aim for.

Yes, it's politics

Many of these devices suggested call for you moving into the political arena and doing what you can to prevent the fires, and to put them out when they get started. But that's the top man's job. Here again is your objective:

1. Keep on top of what is going on.
2. Check communication up and down. Is the message getting through?
3. Determine the cause of any unrest.
4. Figure out how you can put the political activity you find to work for the company.

Now for some plans for cutting down the need for politics.

19

Use Some Creative Management

What's that—creative management?

Here's the explanation as one top executive of a company gave it to me, "Take a known technique and use it to attain your objective."

This man had started his interview by asking, "As the top executive officer of this company, I should be able to teach the men under me a thing or two about politics. Right?"

I agreed.

"And shouting, 'Stop it!' is no dice, right?"

I agreed again.

"So I use what I call, 'creative management.' "

That may sound involved but all it calls for is taking a known technique and using it to curb the politician, encourage him, or slant his efforts to the good of the company.

A known technique! The wonder drug you use to deal with

company politics doesn't have to be new. It's probably better if it is as old as the business—tried, tested, with a good performance record. The executive laughed as he explained, "Let's say you got a guy that spends most of his time politicking. Okay, load him with work, put a deadline on it, and he won't have any time for politicking." Makes sense, doesn't it? Another example he gave was this, "If the politicians are trying to get you to move in on a man or department and straighten things out, stall on it—use passive resistance. In time they may move on to something else."

Another top executive told a story that illustrates this technique. His company had set up a system that had a representative of the accounting department come around each six months and check on the value of company memberships in different trade associations. One day he discovered that his company had resigned from a trade association to which it belonged. The president of the association telephoned to ask why. The company president checked and found the company had resigned from all such associations. He talked to the man responsible and that worthy reported, "I got tired of justifying our membership in those associations to guys that can't find right field in any ballpark. I crabbed about the system, filling out those long forms every six months, and nothing was done about it. So last time I said the hell with all of them. Now that accountant won't come around anymore." The fellow who gave up the memberships was using a technique that we all know, perhaps he was living dangerously, but he accomplished his objective. He got the system changed because he was smarter than the system. How can you be smarter than the system or the men working under the system?

There follows a description of some of the techniques that top executives are using to follow their plans of "creative management." The few mentioned here should suggest others to you that might work on your problems.

Avoid familiarity with subordinates

The other day on a factory trip, my guide called, "Hi, Sleepy." Later he explained, "That's my boss." What this told me was that both the guide and the boss were wrong in their relationship. Every junior executive in your company wants such familiarity with you. You know that so don't encourage such familiarity. Be friendly with your subordinates but never intimate. The other day I heard a retired army colonel give a short talk on this subject to a group of supervisors. "Be the boss," he said, "and don't allow anybody to presume otherwise. If you allow them to get too close to you, they will take advantage of you. If you get too familiar with them, you lose the respect that is necessary in a boss-worker relationship." One executive said, "My boss says he has an open-door policy. I can get in to see him at any time, but he lets me know that the door swings the other way too. He can throw me out just as fast." Perhaps you like to have Archie, the clown, around for the laughs he gives you. But what is the impression on the rest of the group? Does a man need to be a clown to get your ear? Others notice and assume. Check the men you eat with, play golf with, go fishing with. Who shows up at the outside meetings you attend? Does this contact with you subject these associates to political pressure? One president told me of a man in his golf foursome. "He brought me an idea that I'm sure wasn't his. Now I don't know whether or not the fellow who gave it to him felt that he couldn't get to see me about the idea or didn't want to be the sponsor."

Check advice and advisors

Where is your advice coming from? Is it coming from the same men each time? You ask for advice on a matter. One executive gives you one bit, another a bit that is exactly the opposite. Which do you go along with? If one man gets the reputation as the one who advises you what to do, he becomes the target of the politicians. One top man was using "creative management" when he asked, "What will you gain if this is the decision?" A similar question might be, "What will the company gain?" If the man can give reasons he probably has given some thought to his answer. You might suggest, "Check this out with Henry, will you, please?" You may have some men who will bring you good advice each time you need it. Others who don't seem to be able to suggest anything anytime. Then there are those who spar to find out what you want before they suggest their thoughts. Can some of these latter be taught to bring advice in a usable form? One executive said, "I have to check each important decision to see whether I'm making this decision, or somebody else has maneuvered me into making it. The latter may be OK, but I'm responsible and I want to know." To check your advice it might be well to catalog each man—Joe's a "yes-man," Bill's a flatterer, Abe's against everything. Get some of each kind in on the advice, and it probably will be close to right. But don't kid yourself. Ask, "Why did I decide this way?" Whose idea was it?

Watch background influence on decisions

Let's say your background is manufacturing. It is natural then that you might give more promotions to manufacturing men. Perhaps you know them, or you can better appraise their records. But what will this policy do to the company in five years? A few years of this and the top echelons might be weak in other fields of knowledge. One executive, who had come up through accounting, said he discovered that he was making too many decisions on the basis of cost even when other factors should have been given more importance. He found too that each plan presented too him by his executives played up the cost data. "The fellows below knew my failing and so they were slanting all their appeals at my weakness. At times I am sure this was not wholly for the best interests of the company. But this was the way to sell the deal to me. And so I got costs and costs and costs." If your background is not influencing your decisions on appointments or policies, check to see that recommendations made by those below you are not influenced by your background. Ask men with other backgrounds what they think.

How many are trying to keep up?

The other day a vice-president said, "Ed, not too many men are really smart." He was referring to the men in his organization that had been assigned to handle a ticklish situation and had failed. A second man put in, "Yeah, and too many of them don't know it." Here is a job for the top man. Check on which of your men are smart and which think they are when they are not. How many of them are trying to keep up with the times? Remember, training is a continuous process and a man who doesn't read, doesn't attend classes or lectures, can't keep up. It is from the group that is trying to build up that you have to select the men for promotion. If you have too few ambitious men, you have to see what you can do to instill some desire in the ones that have possibilities. Talk to the latter and see what can be done to help them get the knowledge and training they need. One executive put it, "We have a system of nominating a number-two man in every department; I try to know each of these number-two men." This plan gets the data on the manpower pool out of the file cabinets to where it can be used.

Check cost of reports

The head of a company showed me a set of beautiful graphs that illustrated the progress of each department in his company. At least five or six colors were used in the production of the display. "I get these every month," he explained. The exhibit was attractive and it told the story simply, but I asked, "How much does it cost the company to get that report to you each month?" He said, "Not much. One of the boys here does it." I doubt that, "Not much." If he checked on the cost of that report, I'm sure he would have had to question whether or not it was worth the cost. You ask for certain figures and the assistant says, "All right," and goes off and gets them. Next time ask, "How will you get these figures?" and, "How much will it cost to get them?" The answers to both questions are revealing. The man asked to get the figures may be covered over and may have to lay his work aside to go off on this detour. One fellow told me, "I'm working nights to do my own work. The company has gone nuts on this five- and ten-year projection stuff and all day I'm working on estimates of the business we'll do in the dim, distant future. It's all guesswork and all a lot of crap."

The reports may be worthwhile, but, if one or more men have to be taken off productive work to get them out for you, that productive work is certain to suffer. Check the cost, check who is taken off his job to collate the information. Then ask, "Are these reports worth this much?"

Of course, you'll get complaints. But why not have the man who claims he can't operate without the reports make the survey that checks on the cost of the reports? Then ask, "Gus, if these are so valuable to you, we can charge them to your budget, can't we?"

How are reports used?

One top executive made a check on the use of reports that were being fed to his executives. "I started asking, 'Why are these reports issued?' From most of the men I got, 'We've always had them.' Then I asked, 'How do you use them?' Of course, each man quickly made up some uses. But the answers convinced me that too many of them were filed neatly in three-ring binders. And the company makes no profit filing material in three-ring binders." Count the reports that come into your office at weekly or monthly intervals. Estimate the amount of work that goes into them. Then see which reports can be cut without anyone missing them. You might try "creative management" on this. Stop a report without any announcement and see who complains. Perhaps nobody will. You'll save time, labor, and money if you can eliminate even one report.

Check staff buildup

You say, "We're a small company and don't have any staff." But watch it anyway. You kick old Angus upstairs so that you can put a young man in charge of his department. You give Angus a good title and assign him some tasks to save face for him. He needs a secretary, of course, but that is not too expensive. Then he starts a study and he needs some help to do it. You approve, adding one man. Then he branches out in another direction and you approve, adding another man. In most cases both of the men were men on productive jobs. So the staff function has pulled two productive men out of jobs where they were contributing work. And now what are they doing? Studying moon shots or something? In a company with divisions, the staff keeps asking the divisions for data. Some man on a full-time job in the division has to take time out to get the data. And so the staff payroll is not the whole count of how many people are working on space projects. The other day I met a friend who had taken a new job with a corporation. I asked, "What are you doing?" He said, "The headquarters of this corporation has had no staff, now we are building one."

I laughed, "On your last job you were always beefing about the staff people, about them not knowing anything about the business, and asking you for information they couldn't possibly understand. I thought you were antistaff."

"Those staff guys got me fired, didn't they? Maybe I'd be better at getting guys fired than in holding a line job."

A staff may help you and it may not. But check its value to the company and how much of its production is made work. To those below, the staff is you. The staff is power. Most of the line executives are afraid of the staff. A request from the staff is a request from you. Let the staff build up and you will be accused of initiating projects that you don't know are in existence.

Last week an executive told me, "I was recently transferred from a staff job at headquarters to a line job in one of the divisions. On my first week on the job as I read a letter I asked, "What damn fool wrote this? And there at the bottom of the letter was my signature. As a staff man, I thought it a good idea. As a line man, I knew it couldn't work."

Staff means payroll. As you move a staff man to a line job, don't replace him.

Know how to get rough

No matter what kind of operation you run—authoritative, consultative or freewheeling, there comes a time when you have to get tough. Most of the human relations advice covers how to handle workers as they want to be handled. But there are times when you have to bring the group back to realities. Take a small thing like coffee breaks. The ten minutes allowed has extended to thirty minutes. What do you do, cut coffee breaks out completely? And that may be it. One executive told me that he had done just that. "Talking to them and threatening did no good. I stopped the breaks completely. In time a committee came to see me and we settled the coffee breaks, plus getting in late and a few other things." Study the facts, estimate the effect and then let them have it. One executive says, "A blasting does them good now and then."

There will be times when you are tempted to go part way on what you know should be done, but you'll find that these half-way measures are totally ineffective. Get lax on one thing and you'll be inclined to be lax on others. Get rough on one issue and everybody snaps to attention. One office manager said, "We're running a business, not a social club."

"You have to be ruthless when necessary," one president advised. "You have to say, 'The hell with human relations,' and barge in. Being a company president is no job for a sissy."

Another put it, "You can't kid about costs. If you have to cut deep it means payroll. And at times you may have to lay off the best friend or the brother-in-law to make ends meet."

Handle the bureaucrats

When the intrenched try to stall your decisions or block your plans, move in on them. Follow the adage, "Give them something else to worry about. What's the bureaucrat's main objective? To hold what he has, isn't it? OK, suggest taking away some of his power. Ask him to give you a report on why some of the work should not be moved to another department, or eliminated entirely. Suggest cutting the department payroll 10 per cent.

The bureaucrat likes to deliver information in his own sweet time. OK, when you assign jobs ask, "You should be able to have that back here on Tuesday, shouldn't you?" This will put life into a department that usually would take two or three weeks to come up with such information.

The bureaucrat knows he is there to give service. Use this service angle to get him on the ball. A department that takes too much time to get out information is not giving as good service as it should, is it?

Check the growth of such bureaucracies. One executive told me, "A few years ago our accounting department occupied one small corner of a floor of our office building. Now it takes up one whole floor. Oh, I know about figures for the government, and taxes, and cost reductions. But this seems ridiculous. I believe we could fire half of those people and still turn out the same amount of work." Check any of the service departments for this growth. Do you have too much of any of it?

Compromise on small matters

This spreads the impression that you can be sold, that you will change your mind. At times you can give in completely. At others, make it give and take. Check each of these small matters and, if possible, don't be too stubborn. By giving in, you show that you are not against everything, and you encourage the help to bring other ideas to you.

Talk politics with the top politicians

Not to help them with their politics but to show that they don't need to spend as much time at it.

Make a list of the top politicians. Analyze how each is trying to push himself ahead. Let them know that you know what they are doing and understand their motives. Explain that they don't have to spend so much time on these activities. Prove this by analyzing the last three promotions. Show how little politics had to do with any of them. If it looks as if politics helped on any of them, list the man's abilities that got him the promotion. Ask Charlie, "How much company time do you spend politicking and how much working?" "Charlie, you been worrying about getting ahead through politics. Why don't you put a few more licks on the job and see if that won't get the attention?"

One creative management device with cliques is to play one group against the other. One presents a plan. Have the other group present one too. Another is to tell the politicians that you won't listen to such conversation. A third, mentioned before, is to ask for all answers to your "why" questions in writing. These may frustrate the politickers for a short time and may discourage them too.

Build on successes

If the plan worked once, there may be no reason why it will not work again. Check back on the plans that worked well in the past, years ago perhaps. Why aren't you using them now? Many times when I make a suggestion, the man that asked for it says, "We used to do that." Then he may ask one of the others, "Why did we stop it?" Usually no one can explain why a successful practice was dropped. Analyze the successful moves you made in the past, find out what made them tick and check to see how you can use them in whole or part again. An idea may be old but still useful.

Analyze what you have accomplished

The record stands, of course. Claim everything in the press release, shower the congratulations, but don't kid yourself. How much did you or your organization or Tonto, who is shaking hands with everybody, have to do with it? How much was luck, or timing, or some other factor for which you can claim no credit? One executive told of an assignment his boss gave him to explore the possibility of getting one of the largest accounts in his state to handle the company's product. He made one call and arranged to take the account away from a competitor. "I can't tell why," he explained. "The man seemed glad to see me. He asked a few questions, I answered, and we wound up with an agreement. Maybe it was luck, something our competitor had done. Can't find out. But I'm a hero because I got the account." It pays to check all angles of performance. What helped make it? How much luck, timing, company reputation, sweat and tears went into it? Get a few heads together and talk it out.

Confound the credit grabbers

An analysis of what is accomplished will take much out of claims of these men. But without the analysis they will deal themselves in for credit. An executive told of an idea one of his department heads had brought to him. The executive suggested that it be submitted in the company's suggestions system. The idea went in and a large money award was made. Now a worker in the factory who had made the suggestion originally let out a yell, demanded the money, threatened a lawsuit. The union moved in, and there was much excitement.

There are such credit grabbers in every organization. If you have men you suspect, ask them questions such as, "Just what did you have to do with this success?" Many times the credit grabber doesn't lie outright. He just infers. A question that asks him to reveal details will stymie him. A man who tries to steal credit feels that he is smarter than you. Show him you are wise to him, and he may go out and do something for which he should be given credit.

Analyze failures

The other afternoon after the Cleveland Browns had taken a beating from the New York Giants, a reporter asked the Brown coach, Blanton Collier, "What happened?" Collier said, "I'll have to look at the movies first." Too few businessmen have any setup for looking at the movies to find out what caused the failures. Think about this review idea. Ask yourself, "How can we look at the movies of the game?"

Such an analysis allows you to put the finger on failures of men, techniques, product, or plan. And if you know what caused failures, you can set up checks to prevent them in the future.

In checking such failures, put it on a "we" basis. Why did we fail? Not why did Sammy fail? Surely it may have been part of the team that let you down, but go at the examination with the idea that you have missed a few blocks or tackles yourself. Such examinations are "creative" management for you are teaching your subordinates to make such checks.

Stop helping the politicians

The politicians can't do too much if they don't get your help. You may be responsible for more of the company politics than you think. Why not make these checks? Some of them have been mentioned before, but this review allows you to make a quick check on what you are and are not doing.

Are you listening to them? If you do not listen, the politicians may say, "We're not gaining much by trying to play politics with him."

Do you allow the men to try to sell you on them? There is nothing wrong with this. It is natural for them to want to, but let them know that they don't have to do this, that you are aware of their qualifications.

Do you appoint committees to study things? This is making cliques. Give one man the job.

Are you "buddy-buddy" with one man or group of men? When the group meets, how many outsiders are trying to look over the fence and find out what is going on?

Do you wear a lodge pin? Are some of the brothers using this to their advantage?

Do some of your executives have too little to worry about? This may encourage them to take up politicking.

How about your office? Is your secretary partial to certain advisors? Is your administrative assistant using you to get what he wants?

I submitted this list to a number of executives and each of them said, "Not only this, but. . . ." What can you add to the list? If you are doing any of these things, check on which you can cut out.

Think of "creative management"

You may laugh at this idea of "creative management." But try using some of these techniques. The fellow is bellyaching about a policy. OK, ask him to study the matter and bring in a report on what the company should do. He asks himself, "Why did I open my big mouth?" You've been after a man to clean off his desk. He says he needs everything he has on it, old magazines, newspapers, letters, reports, scraps of paper. Some night after he has gone home, move in and clean everything off that desk. Put the litter in a carton back in the store room to give him if he screams. Chances are he will never say one word. Here again are these ideas about "creative management."

1. Accept that fact that you are getting paid to be smarter than the politickers who are out to gain your favor, thwart your plans, or what not.

2. Try some "creative management" on them. Take the wheels off the bikes, hide the roller skates, do something.

3. Check yourself on how you are helping the politickers and stop helping.

Now for some thoughts on an outside help in holding your top spot—the consultant.

20

Use Consultants to Strengthen Your Hold

You might say, "The reason you say that is because you are a consultant."

Maybe so, but top men in companies use consultants and are doing it more and more. There are many reasons why and many devices you can use to keep the consultants on the beam. Because I have worked with consultants as an employee of companies and I have worked as a consultant, I believe that I can offer suggestions that can be helpful. I am sure you have heard most of the arguments why consultants might help you in your work. I select the following from circulars that some of them have prepared.

Why hire consultants?

1. *Outside viewpoint.* It may be that all of your own people are too close to the business to make recommendations on what should be done.

2. *No inside ties.* They are not mixed up in the politics of the company. They may bring you ideas that are not in the interest of any one group or clique.

3. *They have no fear.* They can tell you to do what the insiders are afraid to tell you to do.

4. *Experience.* They may have experience that none of your people have, or have more experience in certain phases of the business than any of your people have.

5. *Can't spare the help.* You have a survey to make or an analysis to do and all your men who might do this job are covered over. It's less expensive to hire a consultant for three months than to put a man on the payroll.

6. *You want backing.* You feel the company should make some moves and are hesitant to do it on your own. The consultant's report says this is what you should do.

How to use consultants

These reasons for hiring consultants suggest two ways to use consultants.

a. *Assign a result.* Get them to make a survey and turn in a report that suggests you do something that you want to do but haven't the courage to do without the backing of the report from the experts. For instance, get a new advertising agency, manufacture a new type of product, change a pattern of distribution, fire a distributor.

You justify this course by saying, "I feel this should be done but, just to make absolutely certain, I want some outside people to check it to see if I am right in my deductions." Here is an instance of this from my own experience.

One company asked me to make a survey of its distribution in Chicago. "We want to confine our distribution to one distributor out there. We got three now. Bring in a report that advises us to get rid of these two. Make it strong too, for one of our board has to be sold." This is laying it on the line for the consultant. If he takes the job, he knows what his report must say.

b. Assign a job. Assign the consultant a job of work on one of your problems. You set up limits but offer no suggestions on conclusions.

Under this plan the consultant would be told, "We got three distributors in Chicago now. We want to get rid of two, check to see which two can go with the least loss to the company." The report here might agree or not agree with the management thinking, but it might possibly be closer to the best interests of the company.

Three checks to make on any consultant

These three quick checks will help you analyze the report of any consultant. Ask these questions:

One, what is his background?

Two, where did he get his information?

Three, how about his integrity?

His background. This is certain to influence his report. If you want a report that has largely to do with manufacturing changes, get a man that has experience in this line. Then try to keep him on manufacturing. Any thoughts he may have on distribution may be helpful but get the most good you can out of what he knows. If you want the distribution check, get a man who has had experience in moving merchandise. The other night I heard a consultant make a talk on distribution. I felt that many of his suggestions were out of line. Afterwards I checked and found that most of his work had been in manufacturing. "When we finish with manufacturing, we move right into the sales department," he said. Some consultants have men with experience in all fields and they send in a team. But check each man assigned. Talk to each, ask a few questions, and you'll be better able to determine whether or not these men should be working on the phase of the survey assigned to them. Keep in mind Minnie Minosa's retort to Frank Lane when the latter was trying to give Minnie some advice on playing left field. "Mr. Lane, what big league team did you ever play left field on?"

His information. In most cases the information in the consultant's report comes direct from the men in your company. The consultants get facts from your men and use them in the report to you. You may ask, "How can these fellows dig out these facts when I don't have them?" This is your communication system. You don't talk to the men the consultant talks to. In one company I worked for a consultant made his office in my department while he made the survey assigned to him. We talked a lot, ate together, discussed problems. In time he came to me with a report. "Here's what I'm going to submit upstairs," he said. "I'd like to have you read it and give me any suggestions." I read the report and said, "This is pretty much what I've told you over these weeks."

"That's right," he agreed. "But what chance would you have of taking that report up to the top office?"

He took the plan up to the top, got it considered, and adopted. I had no complaint because the plan was what I wanted. But I had no line into the top man's office. He did.

His integrity. This is a tough one to check, but you might talk to some of his references. Go see an executive of his client and ask, "Is he the kind of fellow that will tell you what you

don't want to hear?" "Can you mention an instance of this?"
One of my friends, a consultant, was hired by the owner of a
company and was told, "Something is holding this company
back from the growth it should have. I want you to check
this and tell me the truth. What's got us stymied?" In time
my friend came back with his report. He told the owner,
"You're the stumbling block. You are the sole cause of the
troubles around here. Take a trip to Europe for a year or so
and see if these troubles don't disappear." That fellow was
living dangerously, but he was honest. In your interview
with the consultant, let him know that he can bring in this
kind of report if it agrees with the facts. If you want a "yes"
man on the job, check to see if he is a "yes" man. If you want
the truth, try to get a man who will dig out the truth rather
than give you a report on what he assumes is what you want
to hear.

Give the consultants help

Give any consultants you hire a proper field in which to
work. Explain their objectives to the senior executives. Have
these senior executives pass on your explanation to those below. Try for an understanding of what the consultant is to
do. Explain how he might help you. Get over the thought that
the consultant is like a doctor you hire. You engage him,
listen to his advice, but you don't have to take it. Such an
explanation may help get everybody working with the consultant.

It would keep you from being in the position of the company in this story. The company hired an efficiency expert.
The employees got together and decided not to cooperate with

him. When he asked one man what he did, the man replied, "Nothing." He asked a second and again got the answer, "Nothing." When a third man gave him the same reply, he wrote on his pad, "Obvious duplication."

Check the consultant's work

Here are a few checks that might be made on any consultant's job where he was not ordered to bring in a report giving findings you ordered.

Was the information produced available from men or departments in the company?

Were any new ideas brought out, or was this a rehash of ideas that have been bouncing around the company for years?

What did the consultant's work do to morale, scare the daylights out of everybody? Did any promising executive quit?

Did the consultant's work increase the political activity? Were the cliques trying to get their ideas into the report? Did one of them succeed?

What did the work cost? Do you feel the results were worth this cost?

Whose idea was this consulting anyway? Was it yours, or did one of the factions suggest it?

Were the consultants the type that made you feel inferior, or made your executives feel that way?

Consultants can help

I don't want any consultant to feel that what I have said in this chapter is in any way intended to be against his use. Consultants can help and do. But when you are using a consultant, do these things:

1. Check him before you hire him and keep him working in his field.

2. Try to set up the proper climate among your executives so that he gets the cooperation he needs.

3. Use the questions suggested to check on the value of his work to you.

21

Build Your Image to Your Specs

Make it fit what you need.

For your job, your company, your customers.

In doing this consider——

What those above want,

What those below want,

What you want.

A little of all three go into that image you present to your public. But what are your specifications? If you are in a consumer goods business, these may be one thing. If you are in a business that sells its product to industry, they may be different. The distribution of the stock in your company to the public may have an effect, a wide distribution one image, a narrow distribution another. I'd suggest you work up the specification for the image you want to broadcast.

267

Set your own specifications

Each company is different. Conditions are different. Personnel to be influenced are different, factors to be considered are different. You are different. Consider what image you should project on this job and then try to pattern an image of you to fit the job and to get the approval from these people watching you.

Use these PR tools to help

When you have decided what image you want to project, use the tools available in your case to build that image. You might use advertising—publicity—correspondence—the telephone—speeches—community work—the United Appeal—chamber of commerce—civic clubs—the church—fraternal organizations—industry activities—management groups—your industry associations—the government, local state, national—education. Any one of these media can help you build the image you want. Here are some ways:

Advertising

You think of advertising as being used to build the image of the company or the product or service sold. But let's assume you change the whole concept of the advertising the company is doing—perhaps a change in format, or in media, in size of the budget. One president told me, "I put the company in television. Some of the board were against it because of the cost, but now they say, 'He took us into television and it was the best thing we ever did.' " A change in format of the advertising may make the company seem more up-to-date, even a low-budget activity such as a modernization of the trade mark. Customers say, "They have a live bunch over there now." Any such change indicates that a leader is on the job. Perhaps your advertising manager has been advocating this change for years, but you are the one who turned on the green light. That makes you the one who will get most of the credit.

Publicity

Hire a public relations man and get him to build you any type of image you want. Last week one of my friends told me of a story he had read in one of the magazines about the president of a company. Neither of us had ever heard of this man or the company. "That might be a good stock to buy," my friend said. I wondered if that was the objective of the press release. In the operation of any company there is news that the newspapers will be glad to print. They print this because a high percentage of the public are interested in stocks of companies. Thus you can be certain that any release you send out will be used, that is, if it is news. News of a new product, a new plan of distribution, a new building project that explains what this move means to the community in the way of additional jobs gets into the newspaper. Personal items on promotions, suggestion awards also get into print. And if each news story is announced by the top executive officer, you get the credit for keeping the company moving.

The telephone

The telephone call to the man above to tell him of good news about the company shows your enthusiasm. You couldn't wait until he saw it in the newspapers. The personal telephone call to congratulate the field manager on a coup he engineered shows you are on top of things. The telephone call, as has been said before, is better than the note because it is more personal, it is two-sided. The other night at dinner a vice-president excused himself to use the telephone. When he returned he said that he had called a factory manager at his home to congratulate him on a production record he had made that month. "I called him at home because I wanted to talk to his wife too," the man explained. With such calls a top man can help build the image he wants.

Correspondence

I mentioned a scribbled note to a director about some news. This is the type of thing that builds image. A style of writing can give an impression that you are alive or that you are a pompous stuffed shirt. You might sign your letters to acquaintances with your nickname. Or with red or green ink, a drawing pencil. The idea is to make a letter from you different. If it is, it helps build the image that you are different.

Speech making

The executive who can give a good speech gives an impression of himself. The other day in a meeting the man seated next to me asked, "Is this guy really the head of this company?" From the speech he was making, the man didn't seem to have sense enough to come in out of the rain. We both know that there is no relation between the ability to give an acceptable speech and the ability to run a company to make a profit, but your ability to appear before groups is a part of the image you reflect. It might pay you to hire a teacher to help you improve your speaking. A scriptwriter can help too. You want both those above and those below to feel that you made a good speech, left a good impression. For when you speak you are the company.

TV appearance

The other evening on the TV the union leader and the top executive of the struck company came on the air. The leader projected the image of a man who was working in the interest of his members, the president gave the impression that he was trying to gyp the workers, even to a greater extent than the union man claimed. I was for the company man, but I am certain that he made no capital with these listeners. He didn't seem to know what he was talking about. If you have to appear on TV, talk about what you know. Get some coaching on techniques. If it is an interview, suggest questions for the commentator to ask. Then prepare to answer those questions.

Community work

If you are in a small town, you may have to get into this type of image-building activity. Make up a policy for yourself. Will you accept chairmanships? Will you go on boards? What is best for you and for the company? Let's say you agree to take part. Then ask yourself in how many activities? The chamber of commerce, the civic clubs, the United Appeal, the church? Perhaps the man ahead of you on your present job has set the pattern. OK, should you follow this? Then consider your executives below you. How much of this is good for them? This decision takes some analysis and discussion. You know that community work does help build a local image of the company and the executives. It can help build your image. The only harm can come if you do so much of it you neglect the business.

Industry work

Any work you do for the industry associations gets stories in trade magazines and newspapers. If you work as an officer or chairman of a committee, you get publicity. The local newspapers pick up such stories and print them. Through this type of work those above and those below see that you are recognized in the industry. Such assignments take time and you have to analyze the time you spend and the publicity you get. Is one worth the other?

Government contacts

Yesterday I saw a photograph of the President of the United States seated at the luncheon table with some industry leaders. If you are invited to such a powwow, you surely pick up prestige with all concerned, those above and those below. Those below say, "They must think a lot of the boss." One of the directors may have suggested your name and he takes some credit. The others say, "He must be a good man." If you are asked to join a group and make a trip abroad for the State Department, or to work on an industry committee with the Department of Commerce, the resultant publicity gives a boost in your standing. Your report to your associates or peers on the activity emphasizes the honor you have received. Speeches to the service clubs on activities add to your local repute.

Good causes

Today education is much in the news with the campaigns for funds for independent colleges, the bond issues to support the public schools. Any work the top company man does for such causes gives the right kind of impression of him. Leadership in many of the civic campaigns can help in this way— head the committee for the sewer bond issue, for the civic music association. Your name associated with good causes gives a good impression of you and of your company.

General attitude

You don't have to write this out. Your words and your actions show it. Walk through the office smiling and greeting those you pass and you reflect some of your attitude. You are a good boss. This is a good place to work. If you don't see the help, don't speak to them, you don't need to write a book. They know. If you know it all, those below try to find out what you want before they put their pennies in the machine. If you won't listen, they stop suggesting. If you never change your mind, they soon find that out. If you seem to be bubbling with enthusiasm, loaded with confidence or running scared, they sense it. If you take on the tough jobs and won't ask a subordinate to do anything you wouldn't do, they give you credit.

It is difficult to hide the image of what you really are in day-to-day contact. One executive said, "I stay away from the office on days when I am low. I don't want to show myself when I am cranky or irritable." This may be an idea if you have those days when you "should have stood in bed." Your attitude shows through no matter how you try to hide it.

Personal action

The newspaper or magazine story or the TV interview can make you out as anything you want but stage a tantrum before a group and you may tear down what you are trying to build.

One of my friends tells of seeing a judge miss an iron shot off a tee and then throw the club after the shot. "What do you call that," he asked, "judicial temperament?" With one act, the judge destroyed the image of what a judge should be. A judge can do this and get away with it for his public is not in a position to see him throw a club. But the top executive has a smaller public that observes everything he does. He walks through the office frowning, fails to speak to one of the men, blows his top. He is building an image. As the song says, "Every little movement has a meaning all its own." The other fellow's interpretation of the movement may not be what you mean at all.

I once left New York to take a job in a small town. One of the women executives I worked with laughed, "You'll have to be rather circumspect in that town. Everybody will be watching you." There is truth in this. Your public sees you in a bar two or three times and they feel you drink too much. Drive a small car and they wonder about you. Get picked up for drunken driving and all the effort you spent in building an image is forgotten. That woman's advice is not too far off. Be circumspect, careful, cautious in what you say or do before groups.

Silly ideas

By watching your faults, you can prevent a poor image. In many ways management makes the help wonder who has the most holes in its head. One of my friends showed me a series of letters that he planned to send out to all employees. I asked,

"Why do you want to send these out?"

"It's a part of our educational program—they need this type of advice."

One of the letters was on the subject, "A clean desk top indicates a clear mind." The others were similar tripe. "What do they make you out to be?" I asked.

You've no doubt seen these clear desks campaigns. The boss says, "Stop keeping stuff on top of your desks." Everybody puts everything in the desk drawers. The boss inspects and the offices and the desk tops are clear. He feels the campaign is a success and perhaps it is, but what does the help think of a boss that would put out such a silly rule?

Cliché ideas expressed over and over in speeches to the employees tell the help about your mental capacity. One executive I know uses the thought, "We can't build on sand." It leaves the help wondering, "What does he mean? We don't use sand, only metal and wood." But it makes the help ask, "Does he know what he means?" Images are built on such details.

You have lunch at the Union League Club with some other big shots. One of them tells about a "programmed learning" plan that his company has adopted. Another says his company is using it too. You never heard of this, don't understand what it is, but it sounds good so you go back to the office and ride somebody because your company is not doing it. The help say, "I wish he'd eat at the automat," but in a short time you have a programmed learning plan. Remember that the help go along with such ideas because they are your ideas. And they rate you on how you go off half-cocked on such ideas.

You think a man that smokes a pipe is a slow thinker? OK, think what you want but don't make a statement on the idea where anyone can hear. It tells too much about the kind of brain you are.

Image and politics

You might say, "There is no politics in any of these image builders you suggest." Oh, yes, there is. You could build the image you want by producing on your job, but this might take too much time. You might be fired from the job before you got your image built. And so you use devices in this chapter to tell all hands that you are on the job, doing a good job, building the business, satisfying the customers, or whatever your assignment called for. You might try this plan.

1. Work up specification for the image you want to present to those above you, those below, and the general public.

2. Decide which of the public relations tools described you can use in this activity.

3. Use these tools to build your image as you want it with your public.

4. Remember, except in rare cases, you can't hold the job on image alone. You have to produce. The image may keep you on the job longer than you should hold it. But image alone won't make you a success.

Now a final bit of advice——

22

It's Not Easy, Mister

Perhaps all that has been said in the three parts of this book could be summed up in these twelve bits of advice:

1. *Decide what you want.* Decide how far you want to go, what freedom you are willing to trade for that advancement, what you need in the way of qualifications and equip yourself to go there.

2. *Impress the RIGHT people.* This is the objective of all company politics. Impress the power above, of course, but remember those below can help you too. Don't neglect them.

3. *Apply your political activities to your situation.* Use those devices you need in your job in your company.

4. *Respect your competition.* Know them, cooperate with them. Don't knock them. You can help them and they can help you. Perhaps some day one of them will be your boss.

5. *You advance one job at a time.* This is the usual rule

and it is a great help to you in training for the job ahead. As you do a good job where you are, equip yourself for the job ahead. Remember training is a continuous process.

6. *Conform.* You may not want to conform in many of the things you should, but go along. What's the profit in being thought different?

7. *Associate with the RIGHT people.* Upgrade your social contacts. If you associate with the RIGHT group, others think you must be RIGHT. Associate with nobodies and what does that make you?

8. *Join up.* If it pays to belong to a group, clique, lodge, or whatnot, join up if you can. Avoid groups that won't help you advance. Don't comment facetiously on any such groups.

9. *Know what's going on.* You'll avoid many political mistakes if you are aware of what is going on around you. Keep your eyes and ears open. You might be able to fend off moves designed to harm you.

10. *Think of image.* Try in everything you do to give the impression that you are capable, that you have what it takes to hold the job ahead. Don't sound off needlessly about anything.

11. *Be loyal.* Be loyal to your boss, to the company. Adopt the attitude, "My Company right or wrong."

12. *Do a good job where you are.* The wise guys may say if you do that you don't need politics. But don't believe them. You need that good record, plus the type of politics that will help you in your situation.

You don't have to play

You don't have to engage in company politics. You can pick up your marbles and stay out. And, if any or all of these activities are distasteful to you, you may feel like doing just that. But you won't go up in the company that way. This too may be all right with you if you can be happy without advancement. But, if you need to get ahead to be happy, then the advice given will help you.

For the book was written to give you an awareness of what goes on in company politics, and how you can use what goes on to get ahead. Perhaps you knew everything that has been said and more about the subject. It may be that you are using all of the devices mentioned and others to advance your cause. But, if some of these devices are new to you, try using the ones that apply. Top executives gave them to me and recommend them highly. They are tested, they work.

But remember this—you are the key man, your wants and desires come first. If you want to advance, get into company politics. If you are a bit hesitant about starting, have no fear. I'm sure that by using some of this advice you can succeed in company politics.

Good luck and God bless you.

Randall Library – UNCW

HF5500 .H393

NXWW

Hegarty / How to succeed in company politics; the

304900187031–